THE CLASSIC
Indian

MOTORCYCLE

Indian

METZELER
Indian

573

THE CLASSIC

MOTORCYCLE

A History of the Marque 1901 to 1953

JOHN CARROLL

Photographs by GARRY STUART

Published by Salamander Books Limited
LONDON

A Salamander Book

Published by Salamander Books Ltd.
129–137 York Way
London N7 9LG
United Kingdom

1 3 5 7 9 8 6 4 2

Distributed by Random House Value Publishing, Inc.
40 Engelhard Avenue
Avenel, New Jersey 07001

A CIP catalog record for this book is available from the Library of Congress.

ISBN 0-517-15950-3

Acknowledgments
Both author and photographer are indebted to the following for their help in the compilation of this book: Alan Forbes of Motolux, Edinburgh, Scotland; David Hansen of The Shop, Ventura, California; Tony Leenes of Indian Motorcycles of Lemmer, Holland; Mike Tomas of Kiwi Indian Parts, Riverside, California; John Marcoulier and Russell Longey, organizers of The Pioneer Valley Indian Rally; Terry de Smet of Oostburg, Holland, for the photograph of his 1909 V-twin on page 23.

Credits
Editor: Dennis Cove
Designer: John Heritage
Photographer: Garry Stuart
Filmset by SX Composing DTP, England
Color reproduction by Pixel Tech., Singapore
Printed in Italy

Additional captions
1 Illuminated Indian head fender light on postwar Chief.
2 A restored 1915 V-twin Indian.
4 Brett Colson's 1928 Big Chief and Goulding sidecar.
6 Jim Smith racing his 101 Scout at Daytona, Florida.
8 Steve Stephen's Indian Chief.
112 Happiness is a restored and roadworthy Indian.
Endpapers Mike Griffiths' Indian T-shirt, tank and tattoo.

Contents

INTRODUCTION

INDIAN MOTOCYCLES – the Hendee Manufacturing Company deliberately chose the name to signify a wholly American product and for the first half of the 20th century the brand prospered and gained a reputation for technical innovation and quality engineering. The company's history is, like that of all industrial concerns, completely intertwined with the economic and political events of the 20th century; depression, war and boom times all affected Indian as much as they affected anybody else. Even though the company did not operate in a vacuum, simply manufacturing motorcycles was not enough to make the marque a legend. Like their Native American namesakes, it was the *men* whose deeds would ensure the legend was not only made but endured, men whose deeds would be related around the fireside, growing greater in the telling in the time-honored tradition of fisherman's tales. In many ways this book is a collection of those fireside tales. There are other books on the Springfield company that certainly contain more straightforward engineering details; there are those that contain far more information on what each model is like to ride and which models are worth buying; there are books on restorations; and others like this one that are lavishly illustrated in color. But there are few that dwell so long on the men who made Indian great; when their riders *earned* nicknames such as Cannonball, Fearless and Ironman rather than simply being given them by a PR department executive. To an Indian enthusiast names like De Rosier, Franklin and Kretz conjure up images of Indian men ahead of the pack entering a dirt-track turn, elbowing their way ahead on a board-track or screaming down the sands of Daytona Beach proudly flying the script trademark of the Springfield bikes and knowing that the color of Indian Red didn't run.

Left: *Participants in the 1995 Annual European Indian Rally enjoying the sunshine of the Scottish Highlands on a variety of restored solos and sidecars.*

Indian had its other heroes too, such as the US Marine Corps corporal who wrote to *Indian News* from the bloodstained Pacific Island of Iwo Jima to say his copy, full of news that the military Indians were popular with their riders, had arrived and that he was looking forward to buying a new motorcycle when he got home. One can't help wondering if he *did* get back home.

In Europe the Isle of Man TT races are now approaching their centenary and the racers there reach speeds in excess of 170mph (273.5kph) during the race, while in America the famous Daytona 200 is now held in a purpose-built racetrack. Yet when Moorhouse, Franklin *et al* thundered around the bend at Creg ny Baa in 1911 and Kretz won the Daytona 200 in 1937, before the clouds of war temporarily obscured motorcycle racing, neither race was even held on completely surfaced roads. Although their speeds were considerably lower, the riders' achievements were in no way any the less because the motorcycles they were riding were so completely simplistic when compared to the brightly-colored high-tech multi-cylindered two-wheeled machines that scream around the world's racetracks in these years towards the end of the millennium. They were machines which were made from iron, steel and aluminum rather than Kevlar, carbon-fiber and magnesium alloy. With Indian's reputation for innovation and technical excellence through its engineers, including Hedstrom, Gustafson and Franklin, it is both pleasant and interesting to speculate by that same fireside as to exactly what Indian's motorcycles would look like if they had been one of the few motorcycle manufacturers to have survived until the present time. This thought process is especially valid when considered in the light of the racetrack renaissance of Harley–Davidson and also various European motorcycle manufacturers' products despite the overwhelming presence of the 'Big Four' Japanese manufacturers. Harley–Davidson are seeking an upturn in their racing fortunes with the liquid-cooled VR1000 which has been campaigned against the Japanese on the hallowed track at Daytona. Oh that it was racing neck-and-neck with a similar fully-faired liquid-cooled Springfield Indian . . .

Floyd Emde gave Indian its last great run when he brought a Sport Scout home first in the 1948 Daytona 200. Sadly, only five years later the company was effectively out of business but as with all legends the name lives on all around the world. The rumble of an Indian V-twin is music to the ears and just maybe when an early Indian motorcycle is fired up in some enthusiast's garage the ghosts of Charlie Franklin, Billy Wells and Jake De Rosier, not to mention Oscar Hedstrom and George Hendee, smile. When carefully prepared Indian 45 race bikes are wheeled out into the Daytona, Florida, or Ventura, California, sunshine for an historic racing motorcycle event and the pits are full of talk of Class C, side-valves and rivalry with Harley–Davidson, it is possible to believe in time travel. One of Indian's advertising slogans read, 'You can't wear out an Indian Scout'. This book shows how true that was, not only for Scouts but for their other models too. Despite this, the history of the Indian motorcycle is one of both triumphs and tragedies – racing successes but missed business opportunities and fanatical rider loyalty despite mercenary directors.

Indian

1901–1910

HUMBLE BEGINNINGS

THE MOTORCYCLE marque known as Indian came about solely as the result of the efforts and collaboration of two men: George Hendee and Oscar Hedstrom, and their interests in pedal cycles. Bicycle racing was a major sport around the turn of the century in both America and Europe. Often races were held on specially constructed tracks known as Velodromes. The technique of slipstreaming became established to enable solo cyclists to attain higher speeds. They would be slipstreamed by a tandem until the development of pacing machines powered by internal combustion engines. These machines originated in France and usually used De Dion Bouton engines. Inevitably, certain of these pacing machines were imported into the United States. This happened in 1898 and the machines were employed at New York's Madison Square Garden Velodrome in 1899. Unfortunately, their reliability was not all it might have been and they often broke down. For the 1900 season a young man constructed an American-made pacing machine. His name was Oscar Hedstrom. An ardent cyclist, both racer and proponent of the machine as mass transportation, named George Hendee had become involved in bicycling manufacture in the Springfield, Massachusetts, area and subsequently involved in cycle race promotion. This endeavor brought him into contact with the man who had constructed the pacing machine and from this would soon come the Hendee Manufacturing Company and their Indian Motocycles.

Hedstrom was born on March 12, 1871,

Left: *Indian – the founders chose the name to signify a wholly American product. One of the earliest surviving examples is this one with the engine number 268 (below).*

and was christened Carl Oscar Hedstrom although he later dropped the first name, preferring to be called Oscar Hedstrom. He was born, the second of three children, in Smolend, Sweden, and emigrated to the United States with his parents while still a boy. His father gained work in the construction industry and Oscar was enrolled in a Brooklyn, New York, school. He showed enthusiasm and aptitude for mechanics and became a keen bicyclist. Upon graduating at the age of 16 he became apprenticed to a small Bronx, New York, engineering works that manufactured watch cases and components. In this employ he learned the use of machine tools, pattern making, and forge work. After completing his apprenticeship he took work with a number of engineering firms but remained a keen sporting bicyclist. In his spare time he started producing bicycles for racers that found favor with their riders because of their light weight and the quality of construction. This work brought him into contact with the first pacing machines and he is reported to have worked on some of them in an attempt to improve their reliability. From this it was but a short step to building his own pacing machine that would convincingly demonstrate his abilities. The pacing machine was ridden by a then well-known cyclist, Albert Henshaw.

Above and right: *Jules Frohlich is the owner of this 1904 Indian. It is complete and almost original. It is the 667th to have been made by the Hendee Manufacturing Company. The engine is a single-cylinder type that displaces 13cu. in. (225cc) and produced 1.75hp.*

Oscar Hedstrom had married Julia Anderson in 1898 and their first child, Helen, was born on May 10, 1901. In later years, on March 24, 1913, Hedstrom would leave the company almost abruptly after a disagreement with the board of directors over some financial matters. Following this resignation he refused other offers of employment in the motorcycle business and lived on his estate on the banks of the Connecticut River. Oscar Hedstrom died on August 29, 1960, at his home in Portland, Connecticut, aged 89.

George Hendee was born on October 19, 1866, in a suburb of Boston, Massachusetts, into a family of Spanish origin. He became a keen bicyclist and succeeded in winning the United States National Amateur High Wheel Championship in 1886. He held this title until 1892 when he turned professional in order to compete on other types of pedal cycle. After three years as a professional he retired from competitive cycling and took jobs in selling bicycles for various manufacturers. Hendee married in 1894 but separated in 1895. In 1897 he started production of his own brand of bicycle in Springfield, Massachusetts. The area was then at the center of US industrial production and finding both skilled employees and a bank to back him was straightforward. His bicycles went on sale in 1898, being tagged Silver King and Silver Queen dependent on whether they were meant for ladies or gentlemen. They were successful and enabled Hendee to purchase machine tools for more economical

production of certain parts. The motorcycle, autocycle or motorbicycle as it was often then known, was seen by many as the logical extension of the bicycle for mass transportation and Hendee was no exception.

He would resign from the company in 1916 having become tired of the disagreements with the board of directors over policy. He had married his company secretary, Edith Hale, in 1915 and, after resigning, moved with his wife to an estate at East Haddam, Connecticut. He occasionally visited Springfield after his departure and is reported to have been saddened by the decline of the company. He died in 1943 having been an invalid for the last years of his life.

Through their mutual interests in cycling, Hendee and Hedstrom came into contact with each other and during late 1900 agreed to design and market a practical motorcycle for volume commercial production. The Indian motorcycle had its beginnings in a Middletown, Connecticut, workshop where Hedstrom rented some workshop space. He designed an engine based on De Dion principles but of a new design using castings that Hedstrom had cast from his own patterns. The engine was of inlet-over-exhaust configuration. He improved the timing and ignition systems and also designed a concentric carburetor. The timing was crankshaft driven and electrical power was supplied by batteries which were carried in a cylindrical tube

HEDSTROM CARBURETER
HENDEE MFG. CO.
SPRINGFIELD
MASS. U.S.A.
PAT. JUNE 9'05
HENDEE
667

that was fixed to the frame's front downtube. The engine was mounted into a diamond-shaped bicycle-style frame taking the place of much of the seat post. A fuel and oil tank sat over the rear mudguard. Its bottom curved to match the radius and it was divided into two compartments, one for each fluid, and its distinctive shape would gain the nickname of 'Camelbacks' for such early Indians. The oil flowed down to the engine through a sight glass, an important feature because of the total loss nature of the lubrication system on the early engines which the rider had to frequently check in order to ensure there was sufficient lubrication oil remaining. A small canister-type muffler was bolted under the pedal crank bracket. Control of the engine was by levers mounted to the frame which moved a series of linked rods.

In this form the prototype of what became the first Indian motorcycle was tested by both Hedstrom and Hendee prior to being demonstrated to various people including members of the press in Springfield. To show off the capabilities of the new motorcycle it was ridden up Cross Street Hill where the gradient was approximately one in five. It was duly reported at the time that the new machine started easily and accelerated impressively. The steepness of the gradient proved the idea of all chain-drive as the machine was stopped and started while going uphill and immediately showed a good deal more promise than the belt-drive motorcycles already extant. Hendee and Hedstrom's partnership was cemented into the Hendee Manufacturing Company with Hendee as President and General Manager while Hedstrom was Chief Engineer and Designer. The favorable publicity generated by the reports of the new machine in the bicycling press of the time enabled George Hendee to raise $20,000 through the sale of shares in the new concern. With this injection of capital Hedstrom, assisted by some employees, commenced motorcycle production in a converted loft above Hendee's bicycle works. Engine castings were obtained from the Aurora Automatic Machinery Company of Aurora, Illinios. At the time this company were about to start the manufacture of motorcycles and as part of the agreement with Hendee and Hedstrom used the same castings in their machines. These were marketed as Thor motorcycles and the brand stayed in production until 1915.

Left: *The engine cases bear the company name and engine number while the carburetor bears Hedstrom's name. On the early singles the cylinder was inclined backwards (below) and took the place of much of the seat post in the early diamond bicycle-type frames.*

INDIAN
HENDEE MFG. CO.

The first machine was followed by a small batch of motorcycles and to further promote them Hedstrom rode one of these around New England velodromes during the intervals between bicycle races. He made circuits at different speeds and demonstrated turns to favorable public acclaim. Possibly because of the duo's European origins, a 1901 Indian was shipped to England in 1902 where it was exhibited at the annual Stanley Bicycle Show, at which motorcycles had been exhibited for a number of years. Once again public reaction was favorable. Hedstrom continued to give demonstrations of his machine's abilities. He advertised in the bicycling magazines of the day and in 1902 sold in excess of 140 motorcycles. The upshot of this was that by 1903 Indian was becoming a prominent name within the fledgling industry. Although Hendee and Hedstrom perhaps did not know it, in the same year, but in another state, William Harley and the Davidson brothers were starting to produce motorcycles in a similarly humble way and the fortunes of the two companies would become intertwined.

The Federation of American Motorcyclists (FAM) was founded in late 1903 and later developed to become the American Motorcyclist Association (AMA) and the sport of motorcycling's governing body. The coming year seemed to hold great things in store for the Hendee and Hedstrom partnership with increased production being planned and a growing dealer network. Other men were being attracted to the growing and successful Indian marque such as Jake De Rosier who was to make the transition from bicycle to motorcycle racing. Another was Frank Weschler who joined the company in 1905 as both book-keeper and office manager. He was to play an important role in Indian's future affairs. Weschler had been born in Westfield, Massachusetts, in 1879 and educated in local grammar schools. After this he studied book-keeping, accounting and banking and became interested in the motor car. On joining Indian he transferred his attention

Left: *A 1909 single-cylinder Indian which was one of the first batch of three motorcycles – two twins and a single – imported into the UK by Billy Wells in 1909, the year in which Indian moved to the loop frame.*

to the motorcycle and the motorcycle industry and became one of Indian's most loyal employees, ultimately becoming President of the company prior to his resignation during the late 1920s. Weschler is considered to have been a devout Catholic with a sense of humor and a penchant for honesty. These attributes earned him many friends in the motorcycling world despite the fact that he never learned to ride a motorcycle.

In 1905 Indian sold 1181 motorcycles and added approximately 100 dealers to its network. They also introduced the cartridge spring fork in this year which gave the fledg-

Below: *Billy Wells was the UK importer of Indians. He entered the 1909 London to Edinburgh trial on this single-cylinder Indian, seen with his son, George Hendee Wells. Billy Wells received a medal for a perfect score, which he had set into a silver ashtray (left).*

ling machines some suspension for a more comfortable ride and twistgrips for throttle and ignition control. Growth continued in 1906 and Hendee arranged for an attempt to be made on the Transcontinental Speed Record. The record stood at 50 days for a ride from San Francisco, California, to New York City, New York, which had been set in 1902 by George A. Wyman riding a motorcycle made by the Dyke Manufacturing Company. Hendee picked Louis J. Muller and George Holden to make the trip aboard new Indian twins and shipped the motorcycles by train to San Francisco, California, in July. The dealer, George Hopkins, prepared the machines for the journey and the riders left for New York on August 10. They arrived in New York on September 12, having set a time of 31 days, 12 hours and 15 minutes for the journey which was almost 3500 miles (5632km). The new record stood for several years. The new twin was initially available as a 39cu. in. (640cc) road-going model or a 60cu. in. (983cc) racer.

Another notable success for an Indian mounted rider was in the forerunner of the International Six Days Trial (ISDT). It was first run as the Thousand Mile Reliability Trial in England in 1907 and held on public roads with checkpoints to be passed at fixed times. This meant that reliability rather than simply outright speed was the key to victory. T.K. 'Teddy' Hastings, a member of the Crescent Motorcycle Club, Bronx, New York, entered the inaugural event on an Indian Twin and won. He was aided by both the reliability of the Hedstrom engine and the machine's chain drive which gave an advantage due to the fact that the event was held on hilly roads. Teddy Hastings bore all the costs of his entry himself but was backed by the Hendee Manufacturing Company in 1908 when he repeated his victory. Later, Hastings moved to Australia and became an Indian dealer in the city of Melbourne, Victoria. Following Hastings' success in the trial an Englishman, William H. Wells, was sufficiently impressed by Indian's motorcycles to contact the company with regards to becoming the UK importer for the marque. After some considerable correspondence Hendee traveled to England and a formal agreement was reached. Part of this agreement involved the construction of a showroom in Great

Above: *A 1909 7hp V-twin photographed by its owner, Terry de Smet of Oostburg, Holland. The first V-twins from Indian were introduced in 1907.*

Portland Street, London, England. The first shipment of 25 motorcycles sold well later that year and Wells subsequently set up other Indian sales outlets. This effort on the company's behalf led to him being rewarded with a seat on Indian's board of directors which he retained until 1923 when the company was substantially reorganized.

Yet another man who would have considerable influence on the future of Indian motorcycles joined the company in 1907. His name was Charles Gustafson. He too was of Scandinavian extraction although he had been born in Minnesota to where his parents had emigrated from Europe after the American Civil War. Gustafson was a self-taught mechanic and practical engineer and held several jobs in the engineering field. By 1906 he was working for Reading Standard, a motorcycle manufacturer which was based in Reading, Pennsylvania. This company bought its engine castings from Aurora and so produced machines which were not dissimilar to the Thor. Reading Standard were the first American manufacturer to market a side-valve engined motorcycle. It had been designed by Charles Gustafson who then left to work for Indian. He worked with Hedstrom in the engineering department and later his son, Charles Gustafson Jr, joined Indian. Charles Gustafson succeeded Hedstrom as Chief Engineer after the latter's resignation.

A much improved twin was marketed in 1908. A V-twin, it displaced 38.61cu. in. (632.7cc) and had a bore and stroke of 2.75in. and 3.25in. It featured mechanically-actuated inlet valves but an option of automatic ones could be specified. Because the lubrication system was total loss, an oil gauge was fitted which allowed the rider to gauge how much oil remained in the engine. The fuel and air mixture was delivered by one of Hedstrom's own carburetors while the exhaust gases were disposed of through a small muffler mounted below the frame. This item was still of the bicycle-style diamond design made from steel tubing. The rear cylinder of the engine substituted much of the seat post as the single cylinder models and the fuel and oil were still carried in the camel's hump-shaped tank over the rear mudguard. The coil and spark plugs were of Hedstrom's design and a dry cell battery was fitted. Transmission was by roller gears from the engine to the countershaft although a chain-drive option was available. The wheels were 23in. in diameter and the machine's wheelbase was 51in. Like the singles the whole machine was painted in

Right: *An unrestored 1911 Indian single. In this year Indian offered the 'free engine' as an extra-cost option. This was an engine fitted with a clutch mechanism (above).*

Royal Blue as Indian Red had not yet become the standard color scheme despite having been first offered in 1904. Indian twins would predominate their manufacturing from 1913 onward although the company would persevere with singles, believing there to be a market for lightweight, small capacity motorcycles. They were undoubtedly right but somewhat premature and mass exploitation of the lightweight market would not come until after Indian's demise when Honda and other Japanese manufacturers came to the fore.

Indian, having had these early competitive successes, were aware of the positive publicity which was generated by racing and offered for sale in 1908 a racer. The engine was of V-twin configuration and displaced 60.32cu.in. (988.45cc) through a bore of 3.4375in. and stroke of 3.25in. A Hedstrom carburetor was fitted as with the roadster but otherwise the machine was based around the same diamond frame, albeit with a lower saddle, positioned behind the seat post, and a fuel tank mounted along the crossbar. These racers were among the makes that would thunder around the upcoming motordromes which were replacing the velodromes around the United States. Also offered in 1908 were a number of forecar variants. These three-wheelers featured a forward axle over which was mounted a body and was pushed along by a motorcycle engine in a conventional single rear wheel. The bodies varied depending on the type of work they were intended for. One was a small delivery van while another offered a luxurious passenger seat. Indian persevered with three-wheelers. Sidecar options were common and later a three-wheeler with a single front wheel and two rear wheels was introduced for commercial use, known as the Dispatch-tow.

In 1909 a construction engineer, Jack Prince, who had built velodromes, started construction of a larger track for use by motorcycles in Los Angeles, California. It was named the Coliseum and two riders came west to race there, Jake De Rosier and Fred Huyck from Chicago. De Rosier, who was to become famous on the boards, set some speed records. Soon there was a board-track in Springfield, also built by Prince but partially financed by Hendee to ensure there would be a competition venue on Indian's home ground. Equally important was the fact that Indian's line of motorcycles was completely redesigned for the 1909 season; loop frames were brought in to replace the diamond-style bicycle frames and torpedo-shaped fuel tanks were mounted between the upper and lower frame rails while the oil was in a separate tank fitted to the seat post. The rake and trail of the frames were altered in view of the findings from the company's racing efforts in order to offer better handling motorcycles. The chassis of the modern motorcycle had arrived and by the end of the year the company had sold a total of almost 4800 machines. The success continued into 1910 as the motorcycle had now come of age. In the United States the big V-twin was perceived as the way to go and Indian sought to continue producing this configuration in a strengthened loop frame with the addition of their sprung forks which would last until World War II. Other innovations for 1910 were the 'free' engine and two-speed transmission. The former was simply a clutch mechanism but its development shows the increasing sophistication of the Indian motorcycle in a single decade.

INDIAN
HENDEE MFG.CO
Springfield, Mass.

1902 Camelback Indian

This Indian motorcycle is one of the earliest known to exist. It is owned by David Hansen of The Shop in Ventura, California, who is only its third owner from new. It is not entirely complete and has non-original wheels in order that it can be displayed. Its engine number is 268, which Harry V. Sucher dates as 1902–03 and Jerry Hatfield dates as early 1903. Either way it is a truly historic motorcycle and a real link with Oscar Hedstrom and George Hendee, the founders of Indian Motocycles. All Indians until 1904 were finished in dark blue paint.

Specification

Model
1902 Indian
Year
1902
Bore and stroke
n/a
Displacement
13cu. in. (225cc)
Bhp
1.75
Valve configuration
Inlet-over-exhaust
Top speed
25mph (40kph)
Fuel consumption
70mpg (estimate)
Transmission
Single-speed
Gearchange
Not fitted
Wheelbase
48in.
Wheel diameter
28in.
Frame type
Diamond bicycle-type
Forks
Bicycle-type
Weight
98lb (44.4kg)

1911–1920

THE ROAD TO WORLD WAR I

AT THE beginning of this decade things looked rosy for the Hendee Manufacturing Company. After all, work was progressing on an extension to the factory which comprised both the State Street and Hendeeville plants. However, the money for this expansion was raised through the sale of additional shares in the company and the sales of shares had effectively wrested control of the company out of the hands of the founders and into those of the shareholders. Despite this, Indian's dealership network was continually expanding and much racing success was theirs. Highly memorable board-track events include the race held between Charles 'Fearless' Balke and Ray Seymour at Elmhurst, California, over 50 miles (80km). Balke rode for Excelsior and Seymour for Indian. The race was neck-and-neck for the entire distance although eventually Seymour took the win by a wheel length as he tried overtaking on the last lap.

The founders were keen on innovation and marketing a quality product so in 1912 they developed a spring frame – the machine was introduced in 1913 making Indian the first manufacturer in the world to offer rear suspension on a motorcycle. The founders, employed as managers, found themselves beginning to disagree with the board of directors on numerous matters including the cost of the factory's racing efforts, the cost of the best materials, and expenditure on the expansion of the factory. It was perhaps an indication of things to come.

A man who would have great influence on Indian Motorcycles joined the company

Below: *The 1913 Standard of George Twine has a 30.50cu. in. (500cc) single-cylinder engine. The cylinder is inclined backwards and a Hedstrom carburetor is fitted (left).*

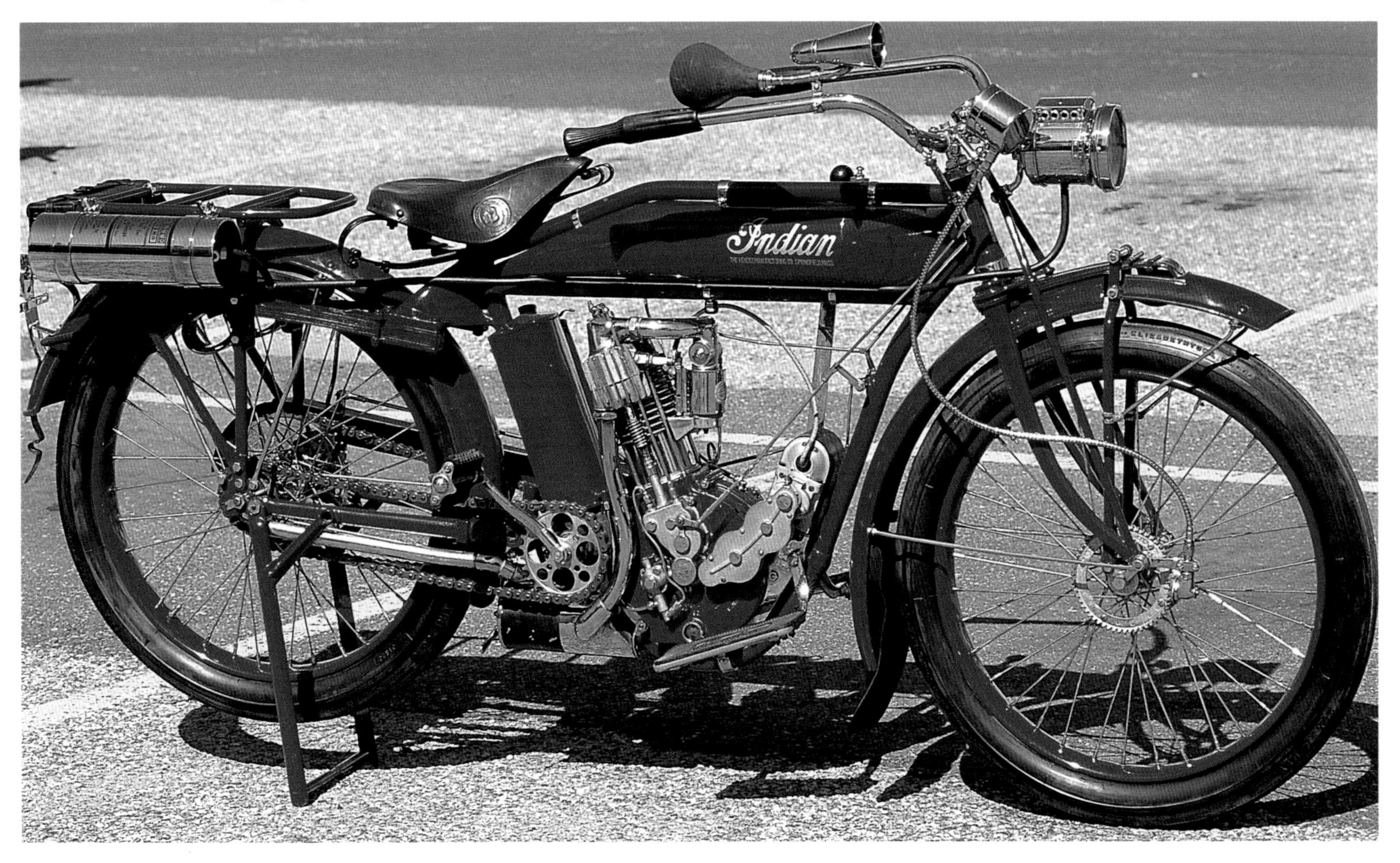

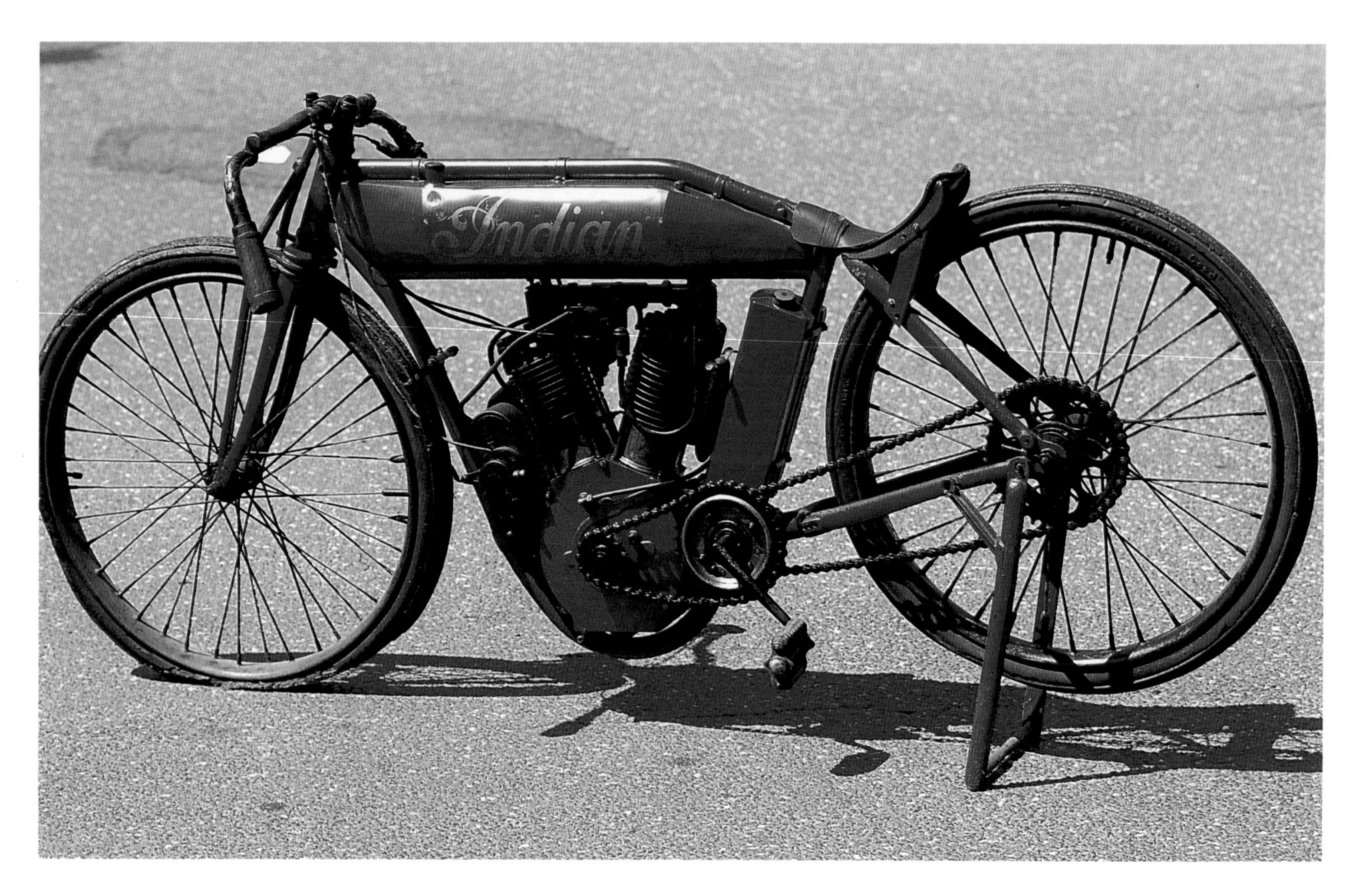

Above: *Donald Harras of Sudbury, Massachusetts, has owned this 1913 board-track racer for 14 years. It is in 'as found' condition but its history is unknown.*

during this decade: Charles Bailey Franklin. He had been born on October 13, 1880, in Belfast, Northern Ireland, the only son of a shipyard worker, Lorenzo Franklin, and Annie Francis Bailey. The family moved to Dublin during the 1890s where Charles attended a school at which he showed an aptitude for science and mathematics. He contracted pneumonia and was seriously ill. Indeed, he almost succumbed to the illness. After a long period he recovered and joined the local cycling club which helped his health by dint of the fresh air and exercise expanding his lungs. Annie and Lorenzo enrolled their son in the Dublin Technical College, a higher education establishment, in 1897. Franklin studied electrical engineering and graduated in 1901. He found employment with an electrical contractor and became interested in the still-infant motorcycles. His career progressed and in 1903 he took a job at a coal-fired power station being constructed on the banks of the River Liffey. Initially he was appointed as Assistant Engineer but in 1905 was promoted to Chief Engineer.

Charles Franklin made the acquaintance of Billy Wells through their mutual interest in bicycles and motorcycles. Interest in the Indian marque increased in Ireland and Franklin competed on one in his spare time. Wells by now had become a shareholder in the Hendee Manufacturing Company and the official UK importer in 1909. (Ireland was included in his jurisdiction because it was not to become independent of Great Britain until 1921.) In 1911 Charles Franklin became famous in worldwide motorcycling circles after being one of the team of Indian riders who claimed the top three places in the 1911 Isle of Man Senior TT. This was the first year that the still-evolving Tourist Trophy races were to use the 37.75 mile (60km) mountain circuit. Racers were required to complete the circuit five times giving a total mileage of 187 miles (300km) – no mean feat. Pedaling gear, which some early machines used to assist their progress on hills, was banned.

Wells was appointed the team manager and requested by Hendee and Hedstrom to find riders to race alongside Jake de Rosier who had been nominated by Oscar Hedstrom himself. Jacob 'Jake' De Rosier had been born in Quebec and taken up motorcycle racing at the age of 23. He made his first appearance in Los Angeles and in 1911 set a record of 92mph (148kph). Board-track racing was a dangerous and dirty sport. It was not uncommon for racers to elbow each others' ignition cut-outs and employ illegal tactics such as hooking, bumping and running a fellow competitor up the track. The tracks themselves were

Above and right: *Indian's early V-twin engined motorcycles were of inlet-over-exhaust valve configuration – the so-called 'F-Head'. Displacement was 38.61cu. in. (632.9cc). Each cylinder and cylinder head were a one-piece casting.*

constructed from boards which were laid on edge and steeply banked. Often they were poorly maintained due to the cost of lumber and the frequency of use, not to mention the oil on the boards from total loss lubrication systems. There were also crooked promoters, and those who cashed in on the risks taken by the riders. It was in such a dangerous environment that De Rosier had amassed a tally of over 900 wins by the time he agreed to race at The Isle of Man.

Special motorcycles were constructed for the TT race which had to conform to a set of rules which included an anomaly concerning displacement. A maximum displacement of 585cc (35.6cu. in.) was permitted for twins

Above: *The Powerplus of 1916 was the first of the new generation Indians, in that they were not designed by the company founders – Hendee and Hedstrom – but by engineers such as Charles Gustafson. The 1913 V-twin (right) was designed by the founders.*

while singles were allowed to displace only 500cc (30.50cu. in) because they were considered more reliable. It may not have been strictly true but that was how the rules stood. For this race the Indians featured 3.75hp V-twin engines. Each cylinder had a bore and stroke of 70 and 76 mm (70 × 76 mm × 2 = 585cc/35.6cu. in.). They also featured chain drive and a two-speed countershaft gearbox. The overall gear ratios were 3.5:1 and 5.08:1 for top and bottom respectively. The racers were designed with a short wheelbase and, in order to incorporate the gearbox and engine within this dimension, the diameter of the flywheels and crankcase were reduced. Otherwise the engines utilizd a range of standard Indian features including overhead-inlet valves and side-exhaust valves, a mechanical oiling system and detachable cylinder heads. The latter components were bolted down with three bolts instead of the more usual four and silencers were not required for the race although they were for practice laps before the racing began. An additional oil tank was fitted on the seat tube with a drip feed. The tank-mounted gear lever was moved forward and closer to the handlebars so it could be easily operated from the crouched riding position assumed by racers. The footboards were substituted by pegs which required a modification to the clutch-operating mechanism. The rear brake was footpedal-operated and the twistgrips turned, one to operate the throttle and the other the ignition advance and retard mechanism.

Charles Franklin was picked to ride alongside Jake De Rosier as were Jimmy Alexander, Oliver Godfrey and Arthur Moorhouse. All the riders were acknowledged to be among the cream of the then current road racers. The five-strong Indian team faced strong challenges from more than 50 other bikes including Charlie Collier on a Matchless–JAP single and Frank Philip on a Scott twin with rotary-inlet valves. The race was not a foregone conclusion by any means and much passing and repassing as well as other dramas occurred over the five laps. G.S. Davidson watched the race and subsequently recorded what he saw in a book entitled *The Story of the TT*. He noted that the day of the race was bright and sunny, meaning that the course was dry, an advantage because much of the mountain course was a farm track which would have been hazardous in wet conditions. Jake De Rosier, dressed in his usual riding attire of running shoes and theatrical tights, took the lead on the first lap. He was trailed by Collier on the Matchless and Oliver Godfrey riding one of the Indians. Franklin and Moorhouse were in fourth and sixth places. The other Indian riders were more conservatively dressed in riding breeches, leather jackets and boots.

The order changed on the second lap when Collier went into the lead. Godfrey kept third place on the Indian with race number 17 despite having stopped for fuel. Jimmy Alexander crashed his Indian – number 7 – injuring his knee and damaging the right hand twistgrip of his machine and Moorhouse moved up to fifth. Things changed again in lap three. Collier extended his lead to almost a minute but Godfrey passed De Rosier. Further down the field Philip, reportedly wearing purple leather to match his Scott, made the fastest lap of the day in a time of 44 minutes and 52 seconds but despite this he was not in the running for the top places. While this was going on Franklin and Moorhouse maintained their positions. Lap four saw major changes at the head of the field. Charlie Collier punctured one of his tires which meant he dropped back to third place and Jake De Rosier broke down in Ramsey. He spent 20 minutes working on the rear inlet valve and changing a spark plug. Oliver Godfrey, on Indian number 26, meanwhile stepped up the pace and took the lead he had acquired to two minutes ahead of Charles Franklin. Arthur Moorhouse, on Indian number 31, stayed in fourth place as the racers went into the fifth and final lap. Charlie Collier mounted another challenge for the lead, passed Franklin and halved the lead that Oliver Godfrey had built up. Despite this, second place was not to be his because he had refueled away from the official points in Douglas and Ramsey so was

Indian

disqualified. De Rosier too was disqualified after struggling into 11th place because he had fitted a spark plug and a nut that had not been carried on the machine. The top three were Godfrey (26), Franklin (17) and Moorhouse (31) with times of 3.56.10, 3.59.52 and 4.5.34 respectively.

The arduous mountain course had taught numerous lessons. As far as the manufacturers were concerned the single-speed race bike was history as were belt-drives. From then on it would be gearboxes and chain drive. The organizers too realized that the differing limits for the varying engine capacities were unfair so, for 1912 when Franklin and others would compete again, introduced flat limits of 500cc (30.50 cu. in.) for the

Below and left: *Unrestored Indians such as these have considerable charm in their 'as found' condition. Indian's innovative engineering can be seen here. The rear suspension appeared in 1913, and the side-valve V-twin engine in 1916 (below).*

Senior TT and 350cc (21.35cu. in.) for the Junior. Indian naturally made much of their spectacular 1-2-3 victory. It remains to this day the only occasion on which an American-manufactured motorcycle has won an Isle of Man TT race.

Billy Wells persuaded Charles Franklin to act as a part-time Indian dealer in Dublin, Ireland. He operated from the basement of the house where he lived with his wife, Nancy, in a residential city suburb. The design of the motorcycle was progressing and Charles Franklin began to work on improved designs in his spare time. He developed a design for a motorcycle with a 'unit' construction engine and gearbox – where the two components were part of the same casting – and by 1912 had worked out the basis of the design that would ultimately become the Indian Scout. His ideas followed those of Peugeot from France who had created mechanically-actuated valves rather than De Dion and Bouton, also from France, on whose ideas most other engines of the time were based. The 1912 attempt on the Isle of Man Senior TT was nowhere near as successful as the previous year. There was no factory sponsorship due to the company being otherwise occupied. Oliver Godfrey

Above: *Later the company regressed to rigid frames (frames without rear suspension) as this Scout from the 1920s shows. Rear suspension did not reappear until the 1930s.*

failed to start due to engine trouble, James Alexander finished in 8th place and Charles Franklin in 12th after suffering from punctured tires.

In the USA George Hendee promoted Charles Gustafson to the post of Chief Engineer. He too followed Peugeot's ideas and, having been employed at Thor, worked on a motorcycle engine that would become the Powerplus for the 1916 sales season. Hendee wanted to strengthen the technical staff at Indian with fully trained engineers. Wells, as a director, suggested that Franklin should be offered employment because of his technical abilities, his interest in motorcycles and his racing experience which made him an ideal candidate. Franklin relinquished his Dublin job and crossed the Atlantic to join Indian. His initial work for the concern was on the Model L which he tried to improve. He then attempted to refine Gustafson's Powerplus engine. He worked alongside Thomas Callahan Butler, an engineering graduate from the Virginia

Military Institute. Franklin designed the horizontally-opposed twin Model O and later designed a 45° V-twin engine that displaced 37cu. in. (600cc). It was an immediate success. At Butler's suggestion the cycle parts featured a shorter wheelbase and smaller diameter wheels than were typical for the time. It was also Butler who persuaded Indian's board of directors about the prudence of moving away from the successful 61cu. in. (1000cc) big twins. The new machine ultimately went into production designated the Scout. It was capable of more than 50mph (80kph), comfortable to ride and handled well. The Scout stayed in production until 1927 with only minor detail improvements and 60,000 machines were sold. It was the Scout that would later be credited with saving Indian from bankruptcy during 1921 and 1922. In 1927 a 45cu. in. (740cc) version of the Scout was introduced which led to the 101 models of both 37cu. in. (600cc) and 45cu. in. (740cc) displacement. The 101 Scout is generally accepted to be Indian's greatest-ever design. Franklin also designed some competition engines and various single cylinder machines including a twin carburetor 61cu. in. (1000cc) V-twin that held the all-time record for board-track racing at 120mph (193kph). Unfortunately Franklin's health was failing. He again suffered from pneumonia and emphysema and died at the early age of 52 in October 1932.

Jacob 'Jake' De Rosier did not return to the United States after the Isle of Man TT races but took part in some match races with Charlie Collier at the famous English Brooklands circuit with the sponsorship of Billy Wells. Collier had set some unbroken records at Brooklands and De Rosier was acknowledged as the US champion so interest in the forthcoming races was at fever pitch. De Rosier prepared a 61cu. in. (1000cc) V-twin installed in the usual board-track frame with its short wheelbase while Collier was to race aboard a Matchless fitted

Left: *Originally, primary cases on Indian engines were painted Indian Red to match the remainder of the motorcycle. Max Bubeck (right) is a longstanding Indian enthusiast who, in 1993, used this 1915 Indian to repeat Cannonball Baker's epic ride of 1914.*

Indian
15
Indian
1990 MEET

Above: *The Powerplus was new for 1916, and the streamlined fuel tank, as seen on this unrestored commercial sidecar outfit, was new for 1917.*

with a JAP V-twin. The two champions were to race over a series of distances: two, five and ten laps with flying starts.

The first race was a close contest. De Rosier allowed Collier to take the lead and slipstreamed him for the majority of the distance, just pulling past him before the finish. He won by a length at 80.6mph (129.7kph). In the five lap race De Rosier tried the same tactic but blew a tire at almost 90mph (145kph). He managed to stop the Indian without crashing but of course had to retire from the race. The third race was also affected by the performance of the motorcycles when Collier's Matchless had a spark plug lead work loose. He managed to replace it while still riding but slowed down and this let De Rosier build up a significant lead. Collier made a determined attempt to catch up but the race went to De Rosier at 84.5mph (135.9kph).

Jake De Rosier was not so lucky after his return to the USA. He raced at Guttenberg in New Jersey where he was in collision with a rider named Frank Hart. De Rosier was not badly injured but Hart broke a leg. At a race at the Los Angeles Motordrome on March 10, 1912, De Rosier was riding an Excelsior and racing against Charles 'Fearless' Balke who was also Excelsior mounted. De Rosier employed his usual tactic of slipstreaming a rider until he knew he could pull out and pass. Balke is reported to have looked over his shoulder as De Rosier made his move. Balke seemed to lose control and swerved across De Rosier and crashed. The motorcycles collided and Jake De Rosier flew through the air and was thrown against the top fence of the track. The famous racer was not killed but severely injured and had to undergo two major operations in Los Angeles hospitals before he was well enough to return to Massachusetts to convalesce.

During this period he campaigned for improvements to the sport including the introduction of rules requiring helmets and goggles for racers, rules to keep novices and intoxicated riders off the tracks, and higher fences, although he would not live to see such things implemented. Still unwell in Springfield, almost a year later he had to undergo another operation. He died on February 25, 1913, from complications which had set in during surgery. His death shocked the American motorcycling world. One newspaper in paying tribute to him wrote, 'There was but one Jake De Rosier. There will never be another, for the conditions under which he achieved fame will never return'. It was true. His death (and the horrific deaths of six spectators and two riders – Ray Seymour and Indian rider Eddie Hasha – at a race in Newark, New Jersey, in September 1912) turned audiences away from the motordromes. In addition, the onset of World War I, the rising cost of timber from which to build the tracks, and the oncoming Depression all caused the demise of board-track racing. Alongside these spectacular triumphs and tragedies Indian were still manufacturing motorcycles but other dramas were being played out behind the scenes. Although they were less public they would have great bearing on Indian's fortunes. So too would the dramas which were unfolding on the world's stage.

Oscar Hedstrom resigned from the company on March 24, 1913, for reasons of his own but which are generally acknowledged to have been as a result of his becoming tired of disagreements with the board of directors over financial matters and in particular a scheme to sell further shares in the company. The directors were not motorcycle enthusiasts in any shape or form and simply regarded the Hendee Manufacturing Company as a way of making money. It is easy to envisage Hedstrom as an engineer proud of his trade finding this situation disagreeable. After his resignation he went to live on his estate in Connecticut and refused a number of lucrative offers of employment with other companies. His departure from the company was undoubtedly a major loss.

The United States attempted to remain neutral in World War I which was seen by many as a distinctly European affair. However, after the sinking of the Blue Ribband holder, the liner *Lusitania*, by the German U-boat U-20 off The Head of Old Kinsale, Ireland, with the loss of 1198 lives in 1915, and the torpedoing of non-combatant shipping in the Atlantic, sympathy was aroused for the Allied cause and ultimately brought the United States into the war on the side of the Allies. From the point of view of Indian and numerous other manufacturers of every type of motor vehicle there was the prospect of sales to the military. It was no secret that the War Department had been experimenting with automobiles as a result of the war with Mexico that had begun in 1914 and led to the American occupation of Vera Cruz. The Mexican revolutionary Pancho Villa had learned to ride an Indian during a period of exile in the United States and had realized the possibilities of using motorcycle riders as messengers in his forthcoming campaign against the Mexican Federal forces in Northern Mexico.

The significance of the 1914 Mexican war was that it was the first time that the US Army had used motor vehicles. Up until this time military thinking on mobility had relied on cavalry. The tactics were those of the American Civil War of 50 years earlier. Indian, and other motorcycle manufacturers, were requested to adapt motorcycles for military use including building three- and four-wheeled machines capable of having machine guns mounted on them. At least one such machine was tested at the New York Armory in 1916.

Below: *This Indian catalog dates from 1917 when the range included the Powerplus and the Model O. It is typical of advertising material of the time.*

Negotiations with military procurement agencies continued in the autumn of 1916 because, in addition to specially adapted machines, the government required solo and sidecar machines. Machines from Indian, Harley–Davidson and Excelsior were tested and eventually Indian gained a contract to supply 20,000 machines and the other manufacturers considerably smaller numbers. It was the supply of these machines that caused significant problems for their manufacturer largely because of the price asked of the army's purchasing agents. The US Army expected to buy their motorcycles, and every other commodity, at the lowest possible price. Indian's board of directors settled for $187.50 for each motorcycle and $47.00 for

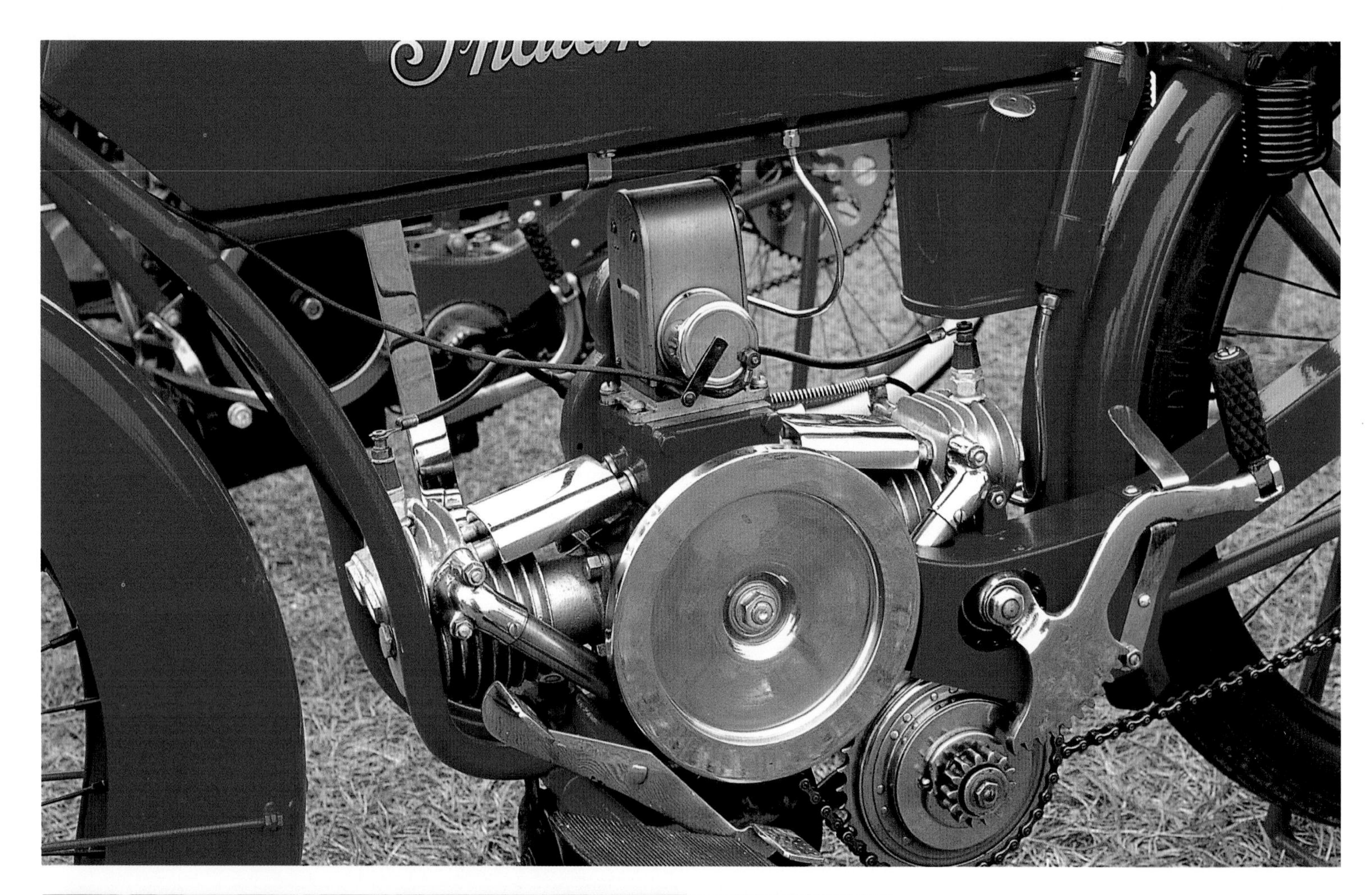

Left: *The Model O Indian was based on the English Douglas. It was an attempt to market lightweight motorcycles and these were made between 1917 and 1919. The example shown dates from 1917 as it has cartridge spring forks – later bikes used leaf springs. The engine (above) displaced 14cu. in. (257cc).*

each sidecar frame and body. The root of the problem was that the costs of materials were increasing considerably due to inflation and the management staff charged with costing out the price of machines for the military contract seem to have considerably underestimated their real costs. As a result the machines to be supplied to the US Army would leave Indian with a significant loss. This less-than-ideal situation forced Indian to look very carefully at its methods of production and the result of this was that a number of specific jobs were sub-contracted to specialists including engine castings which were from then on manufactured by Brown

Above: *Another earlier lightweight motorcycle from Indian was the Model K of 1916. It was only available in that year as a 13.50cu. in. (221cc) two-stroke single.*

and Sharpe of Providence, Rhode Island. Other components were made by the Moore Drop Forge Company to whom part of the Hendeeville plant was eventually sold.

There is no doubt that the Indian factory was in a mess to the extent that General Manager, Frank Weschler persuaded Oscar Hedstrom to return on a temporary basis to Springfield to put things in order again. He was reluctant to do so but agreed and subsequently returned for three months. It was widely seen as his contribution to America's war effort and employee morale rose. What Hedstrom did was to attempt to improve the efficiency of production to the extent that the manufacture of the military bikes did in fact result in a tiny profit per machine. He also cut back Model O production. The military contracts were considered to be less than desirable by this stage as the volume required starved showrooms of civilian models and allowed Indian's competitors to gain an advantage in the domestic market.

America declared war on Germany and its allies on April 6, 1917, despite the US military not being as well prepared as might have been expected. The Democrat President, Woodrow Wilson, made a plea to industry requesting all-out production and as a result output of military motorcycles reached an all-time high. The machines supplied to the military required servicing under field conditions and an Indian employee, Tommy Butler, set up a service organization within the US Army. Through the help of the recruiting agency a total of 3000 mechanics were recruited to continue their trade in the Army. These mechanics also serviced the Excelsiors and Harley–Davidsons in use by the army.

A further and more profitable contract for more machines was negotiated in the spring of 1918 and at the cessation of hostilities the US Army and other agencies owned 70,000 motorcycles. Of this figure, 41,000 were Indians and the remaining 29,000 comprised Harley–Davidsons, Excelsiors and Clevelands. Despite this volume of production Indian were in a precarious position financially and had to face the loss of dealers who had been starved of stock and spares. They also faced inflation. The priority was to get a range of motorcycles on sale to the public for 1919. The range consisted of the V-twin Model N and its electrically-equipped variant, the Model NE. There was also a single cylinder commercial model which displaced 33.50cu. in. (550cc) which was intended to pull a sidecar chassis fitted with a box body. Many of the latter went for export. In England Billy Wells resumed the import of Indians and in Holland a company called R.S. Stokvis and Zonen of Rotterdam took on distribution for much of Europe.

1920 Indian Powerplus

When the Powerplus was introduced in 1916 it was big news simply because of the valve configuration in the engine. Side-valves had caught on in Europe earlier but only Reading Standard were using them in the USA where they had been developed by Charles Gustafson. He moved to Indian and designed a similar type of side-valve engine for the Springfield company. The new engine was noticeably more powerful than the earlier inlet-over-exhaust type.

Specification

Model
Indian Powerplus
Year
1920
Bore and stroke
3.125 × 3.96875in.
Displacement
60.88cu. in. (997.6cc)
Bhp
18
Valve configuration
Side-valve
Top speed
62mph (100kph) (estimate)
Fuel consumption
35mpg (estimate)
Transmission
Three-speed
Gearchange
Hand-shift
Wheelbase
59in.
Wheel diameter
22in.
Frame type
Cradle spring
Forks
Leaf sprung
Weight
400lb (181kg)

Indian
Land of Lincoln
Dec 94
13 463 AV
ILLINOIS

1921–1930

TOWARD DEPRESSION

THE HENDEE Manufacturing Company entered the 1920s in a downbeat mood because of the legacy of the unprofitable army contracts and the loss of many dealers and customers. Added to these problems was the fact that the US domestic motorcycle market was shrinking and Indian's workforce were seeking wage increases. On a national level the unpopular 18th Amendment to the US Constitution was in effect which prevented the sale and production of alcohol. It had been introduced in January 1920 and started what became known as the Prohibition Era. The new Indian Scout model was proving popular both at home and overseas and the model was equipped with electric lights, illuminated by a battery and Splitdorf generator, for the 1921 sales season. The popularity of this model encouraged dealers to clamor for a larger capacity machine of a similar type and eventually design work began on the motorcycle that would become the Chief. It was announced in the fall of 1922 as featuring a 42° V-twin of 61cu. in. (1000cc) displacement of unit construction. While some Powerplus or Standard components were utilized, other major parts such as the frame were completely new. Redesigned mudguards and fuel tank gave the bike a more modern appearance. The Scout, which had been introduced in 1919 for 1920, and the Chief are considered to have been Charles Franklin's best designs. The Scout was both powerful and reliable and gave the Indian factory an advertising slogan, 'You can't wear out an Indian Scout'. The 1920 Scout featured a

Below: *The Indian Chief was produced during the 1920s as was the Prince (left). These models were aimed at different sectors of the motorcycle market.*

side-valve 42° V-twin engine that through a bore and stroke of 2.75in. and 3.0625in. respectively gave a displacement of 36.4cu. in. (596cc) although it was always referred to as a 37cu. in. machine. The engine produced 11bhp. Primary drive was unconventional consisting of a series of helical gears. It was noisy but would outlast the motorcycle and remained as a standard feature of Indian motorcycles until 1933. A three-speed hand-shift transmission enabled the Scout to reach a top speed of approximately 55mph (88.5kph) and return around 50 miles per gallon. The seat height was 28in. while the wheelbase was 54.5in. and the diameter of the wheels was 20in. Ready to ride the bike weighed in at 340lb (154kg). The 1922 Chief was immediately marketed as suitable for sidecar duties in view of its 61cu in. (1000cc) engine. The Chief retailed at $435.00 and featured as standard a spur-driven generator mounted at the front of the crankcases and electric lights as standard. Ignition was by means of a Splitdorf magneto and the battery was mounted between the rear mudguard and gearbox. The Chief could turn 70mph (112kph) when attached to a sidecar and folklore has it that the Chief in sidecar guise was a popular choice of transport for bootleggers involved in running illicit spirits.

The popularity of motorcycle racing took a downward turn in the early 1920s. A number of racers' deaths were partially to blame. Bob Perry, who rode for Excelsior, was killed in an accident while testing an overhead-camshaft racer for the company at the Ascot Speedway in Los Angeles, California, on January 4, 1920. Ignatz Schwinn cancelled all his company's racing efforts immediately afterward. Indian and Harley–Davidson were still involved however and set out to contest the 300-mile (482km) National in Dodge City, Kansas, on July 4, 1921. Indian had seven riders mounted on Franklin's Powerplus derived side-valves known as pocket-valves. Harley–Davidson entered Ralph Hepburn on an eight-valve machine and five other riders on twin-cam pocket-valve Harleys. A privateer, Waldo Korn, entered the race on an Excelsior. The victory, in what was the last-ever Kansas 300-miler, went to Hepburn and Harley–Davidson. A short time afterward Harley–Davidson too would retire temporarily from racing. The board-track phenomenon had not entirely passed and races were still being promoted. There were still enough reckless 'devil may care' riders about to risk all out on the boards and large crowds still came to watch their exploits and also to sample

Below: *The 1924 model Big Chief still contained a number of Powerplus parts such as the one-piece cylinder and head castings. This bike is owned by Donald Haras.*

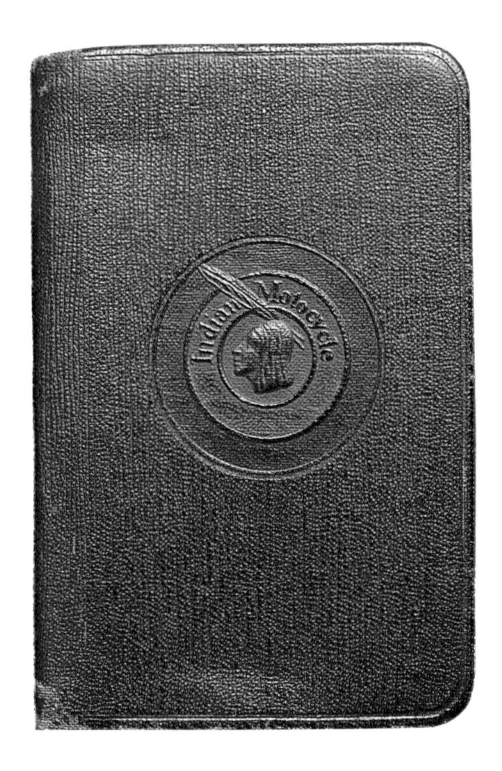

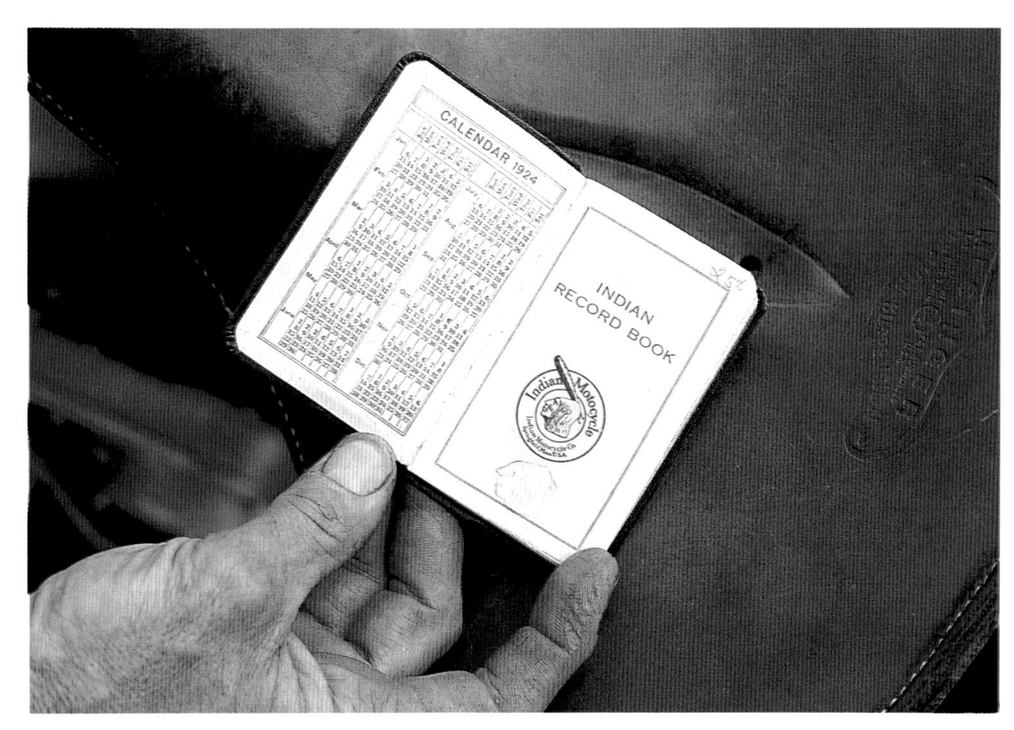

Above: *An interesting item of collectable Indian ephemera is this diary/notebook which dates from 1924 and features the Indian Motocycles logo.*

other attractions at the races. It has been reported that prostitutes openly solicited the crowds, illegal betting went on and bootleg liquor was to be found on sale. Understandably, the transitory nature of the racers' lives and the excitement that the events would bring to town would encourage uproarious behavior. One group of racers who arrived in Chicago to race at the Riverview Park Motordrome are reputed to have pooled their money and rented an entire brothel for the three days prior to the race. There are those who feel that the danger and correspondingly high accident rates led to motorcycling as a whole being perceived in a negative way which, in turn, contributed to the decline in sales, especially when the press began referring to the Motordromes as 'Murderdromes'.

While Indian were still interested in promoting their motorcycles through racing, the effect of such promotion was lessened with both the Harley–Davidson and Excelsior factories not racing. Indian reduced their budget for racing and competition motorcycling of this type went into decline. Charles Gustafson Jr. oversaw racing efforts during this period. Albert 'Shrimp' Burns, Charles 'Fearless' Balke and Paul Bower, the latter too young to have earned a nickname, were all killed in separate racing accidents at Toledo, Ohio, Hawthorne, Chicago and Toledo, Ohio, respectively. Hillclimb competition increased in popularity and Indian riders achieved some endurance records. Cannonball Baker rode an Indian Scout from New York City, New York, to Los Angeles, California, in 179 hours and 28 minutes. Over the 3368 miles (5420km) of the journey he used 40 gallons of gasoline and five gallons of lubricating oil. He averaged a speed of 20mph (32kph). The 300-mile National was held in Wichita, Kansas, in 1923 and it was won by M.K. 'Curly' Fredericks on a 61cu. in. (1000cc) Indian. Overseas, Freddy Dixon entered the Isle of Man TT on a special 500cc (30.50cu. in.) Indian side-valve. He placed third in what was Indian's last TT appearance. Dixon later won the Belgian Grand Prix on the same machine.

Problems in Springfield worsened in 1922; because of the decline in sales the management were in the unenviable position of trying to guess how many motorcycles to build. This precarious situation was worsened by the size of stockholding of raw materials and components due to earlier inaccurate estimates. The banks were becoming wary of the company's financial position and Frank Weschler, the General Manager, tried to resolve the problems. Clashes of personalities between old-time and newer management employees hampered his efforts as did labor-relations problems. One glimmer of hope was that although the domestic market for Indian's products was in decline, the demand from overseas was still strong so that 50 percent of all production was being exported, most especially to areas such as Australasia and South Africa. Despite this, 1922 has to be considered a disaster for the company as it lost more than $1.25 million. Weschler's efforts did pay off because the company made a small profit in 1923 and its export markets remained strong. In addition, South America became a worthwhile market for the company.

The upturn caused the board of directors to reorganize and rename the company. It became The Indian Motocycle Company. (It is believed that the 'r' was dropped to avoid copyright and patent problems.) In this reorganization, the company went public and offered its stock on the Wall Street Stock Exchange. Despite the general prosperity enjoyed by the USA in 1924, the year indicated a still-declining domestic market for

motorcycles: Henderson Fours were being produced in smaller numbers; Ace were in serious difficulties financially; and Excelsior had cut back their production. The main reason for this was nothing to do with bad publicity about motorcycle racing or the salacious goings-on at racetracks but the availability of the cheap mass-produced car. A Model T Ford was by now cheaper than a sidecar outfit. Law enforcement agency sales continued to be important to Indian as did export sales but would not last due to prevailing economic conditions. Another major setback came in 1925. In Great Britain, Winston Churchill, the Chancellor of the Exchequer of the Conservative government under Prime Minister Stanley Baldwin, levied a 33 percent import tax against all foreign motorcycles imported. This pushed up the retail price of American motorcycles to such a high level that they became uncompetitively priced. Billy Wells, who had been the Indian importer for 16 years, ceased his operation. A similar tax was introduced in the Australasian markets in 1929 as the governments of those countries sought to protect their domestic food producers from cheap exported American foodstuffs. The tax was levied on everything so shipment of Indian motorcycles stopped within weeks of the tariff's introduction. South Africa and South America, however, continued to be worthwhile overseas markets.

How much simpler times were in the 1920s is well illustrated by the checkered career of Joe Petrali who briefly rode Indians and later became one of Harley–Davidson's star riders and won the National Championship for them in 1925. He was born in San Francisco, California, in 1904 and became interested in motorcycles as a boy. His first machine was a belt drive Flanders bought at the age of 12 and he purchased a second-hand Indian from Jud Carriker's Santa Ana, California, dealership in 1920. On this he raced against the powerful Harley team on the Fresno, California, board-track. The Harley riders boxed him in but he fought his way out and took second place. Such a daring ride earned him a place riding a borrowed Harley in another big race. He won and so earned a place on the Harley–Davidson team. Later Harley temporarily retired from racing and Petrali managed to obtain a ride with Excelsior. It was on an Excelsior that he broke three national speed records while qualifying for an event in Altoona, Philadelphia. He also won the main 20-mile (32km) race of the event itself on July 9, 1926. When Excelsior retired from motorcycle racing Petrali went back to Harley–Davidson with whom he stayed through the Depression. In 1936 he rode an overhead-valve Harley Knucklehead to a new record on Daytona Beach – an Indian machine held the previous record. The Knucklehead was clocked at 136.183mph (219.164kph), an American speed record and a world record for a non-supercharged engined motorcycle. Later he retired from racing altogether and went to work on Indianapolis Cars and then to work for the eccentric industrialist, Howard Hughes. Petrali flew with Hughes in the one and only test flight of the Spruce Goose, Hughes' massive and cumbersome flying boat, at Long Beach, California.

In September 1926, at a race meeting at

Right: *Mark Johnson's Big Chief dates from 1926. Its engine (left) displaces 74cu. in. (1200cc). As a model it was made between 1923 and 1927, having evolved from the Powerplus. It was gradually upgraded with removable cylinder heads and a new tank.*

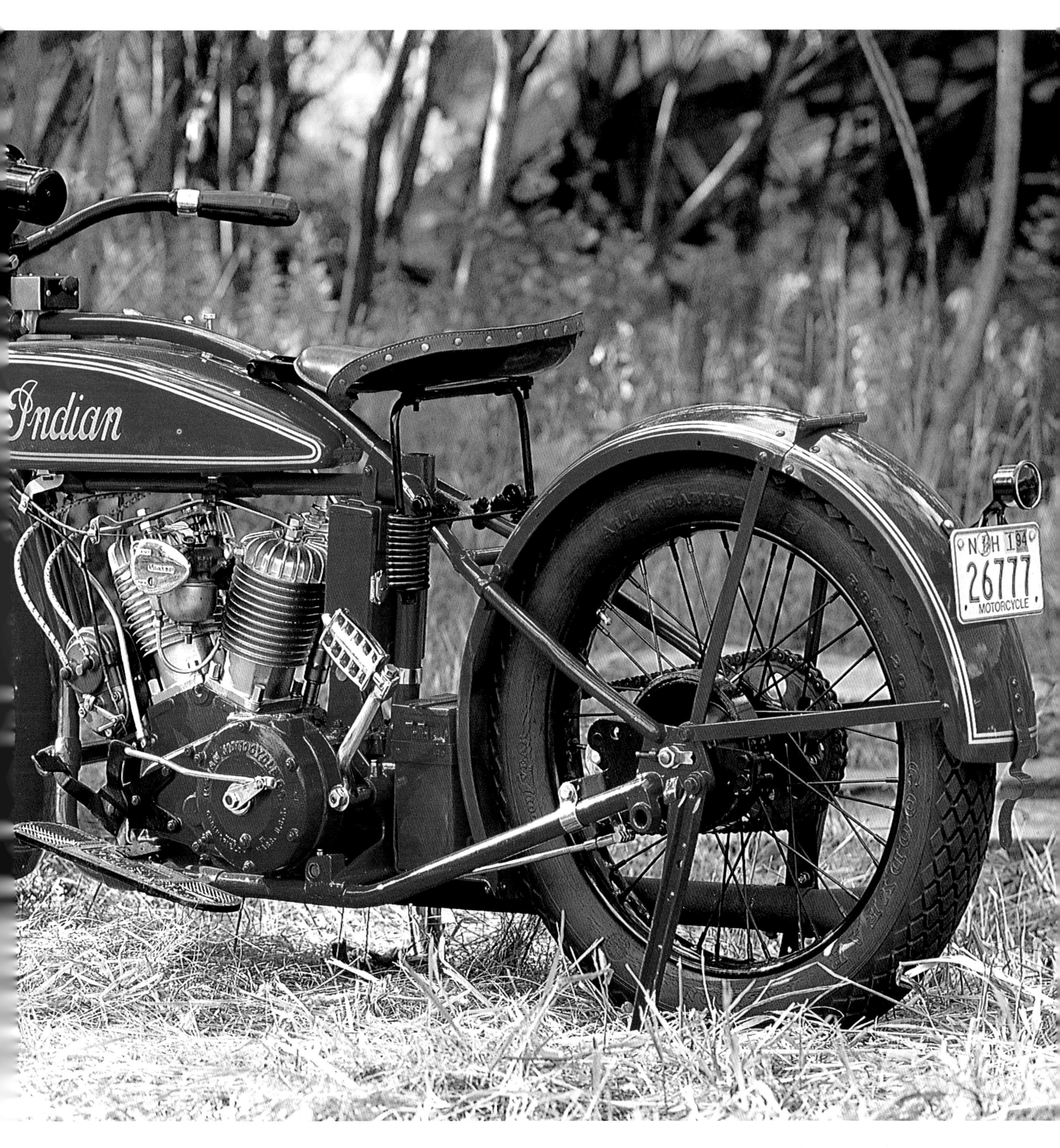
Indian
26777
MOTORCYCLE

Indian
SCOUT
49

1926
Indian
SCOUT
BUTCH BAER
49
Ontario

the oval track at Syracuse Fairgrounds, New York, Johnny Seymour, riding a 30.50cu. in. (500cc) special Indian, set four world records and won three National championships beating, amongst others, the famous Petrali. Later in the same month Seymour broke three more records while racing at a track in Michigan. These race wins boosted Indian's reputation and no doubt helped sales, meaning that the company made a healthy profit for 1925. Seymour also set two new records on Daytona Beach, Florida, in the spring of 1926. The single cylinder 30.50cu. in. (500cc) record of 115mph (185kph) and the twin-cylinder record of 132mph (212kph) were achieved by changing engines in the same motorcycle between record attempts. The twin-cylinder record eventually fell to Petrali on a Knucklehead Harley ten years later. In the later 1920s someone devised the 'stroker' motor for a Scout. The idea behind this tuning modification was simply that by increasing the stroke of the piston, displacement was increased and consequently power and speed. To build a stroker Scout at this time required careful reassembly of a Scout engine with Chief flywheels and crankpin. These though were of too large a diameter to fit Scout cases so had to be turned down but once this was done they fitted and increased the stroke because of the longer throw crank. While it did require a pair of custom pistons it gave a displacement of 57cu. in. (935cc) and a phenomenal increase in power, acceleration and top speed. These modified Scouts were potent hillclimb and race bikes, often in the hands of privateer riders. The custom pistons are reputed to have needed frequent replacement because of their short skirts. They rocked and wore quickly. However, the side-valve configuration of the engine permitted swift replacement. Motorcycles which came from Excelsior, Indian and Harley-Davidson with a displacement of 45cu. in. (740cc) led to the American Motorcyclist Association forming Class C to allow these machines to compete.

The lightweight Model L Indian Prince was introduced in 1925 and retailed at $185.00. It was a small capacity, 21.25cu. in. (348cc) displacement motorcycle and was introduced because many people involved with motorcycling believed there was a market for lightweight motorcycles. They were right but the demand would not be really evident until after World War II. The bike was comprehensively restyled for 1926 to give it the appearance of the Indian Scout and Chief models albeit smaller. It was anticipated that the Prince would be popular in Britain until the introduction of the import tariff. It stayed in production until 1928 with minor upgrades.

Frank Weschler had been made President of the company and given a seat on the board of directors in 1923. This boosted morale at the company in view of his popularity. It was under Weschler's management that Indian acquired the Ace Company, manufacturers of a Henderson-designed

Above left: *Butch Baer on his 1926 Scout in the AHRMA event at Daytona, Florida. The same Scout in the pits in race trim (below left) can be compared with a standard model (below). This model was superseded by the 101 Scout in 1928.*

four-cylinder motorcycle. Ace were acquired by Indian in December 1926 and the first Indian Fours were simply Ace Fours painted in Indian Red with an Indian script logo on the sides of the tank as well as an Ace badge. Perhaps the biggest news though from the middle of the decade was the introduction of the 101 Scout. The Scout had been introduced in 1920 and given new mudguards in 1926 but it was completely redesigned for 1927. Charles Franklin redesigned the Scout by lowering the seat post and frame to give a seat height of only 26in. The wheelbase was lengthened to just over 57in and although the existing design of forks were retained, rake and trail were altered to enhance handling. The altered frame required a redesigned fuel tank, a front brake was fitted, and the engine cases redesigned to strengthen the part that mounted to the frame. The redesigned machine was known as the 101 Scout and became possibly the most famous Indian ever. Its handling and performance were legendary. With its 42°

Left and right: *The Indian Prince was a lightweight motorcycle introduced in 1925 and intended for younger and novice riders. It featured a 21cu. in. (344cc) engine and was capable of speeds of up to 50mph (80kph). This example was manufactured in 1926 and has been restored by Pete Bollenbach of East Dundee, Illinois.*

side-valve V-twin engine displacing 45cu. in. (740cc) through a bore and stroke of 2.875 × 3.5in. it produced an estimated 18bhp and was capable of speeds of more than 70mph (112kph) in stock form. Tuned for racing, with ported valves and hot cams, it could be encouraged to exceed speeds of 100mph (161kph). Transmission remained three-speed and, weighing in at 370lb (168kg), the 101 Scout would return around 50 miles per gallon. A 37cu. in. (600cc) version was sold, aimed primarily at those riders who sought greater economy. The 101 endeared itself to the traveling carnival 'Wall of Death' acts as well as to aspiring racers and most other enthusiastic riders.

When the 101 went on sale it did so with-

Below: *The first Indian Fours were referred to as Indian Aces because Indian had, in 1927, acquired the assets of the Henderson brothers' Ace Motorcycle Company.*

out Frank Weschler as President of the company. The board of directors wanted to speculate with the surplus that had been accrued under Weschler's management. They intended to form another company and trade in the shares of other industrial concerns. Weschler was very much opposed to such a course of action because of his loyalty to the company and his realization that new machinery was required. The board of directors overruled him so on August 27, 1927, he resigned. Weschler died at the young age of 56 in early 1935 when his health failed. He was replaced by Louis J. Bauer, an industrialist. He had, with two others on the board, purchased sufficient shares to give the threesome control of the board. Bauer appointed his son, Jack, a engineering graduate, to a position in the engineering department and while the two had an interest in producing motorcycles they also intended to diversify the company into the manufacture of other things. These would include lightweight cars powered by 74cu. in (1200cc) Indian Chief engines and later patent car shock absorbers. Sadly for Indian neither was successful and lost the company money. Against a background of a seemingly disinterested factory, many dealers resigned their franchises but the 101 Scout continued to sell well.

In these years the American agricultural business was struggling with overproduction of foodstuffs and Congress was pressured to enact legislation to protect agriculture. The Bill, known as the McNary-Haugen Farm Bill, won popular support and passed both houses of Congress but was vetoed for three successive years by President Coolidge who did not favor Government intervention in business. The Bill was signed into law by President Herbert Hoover, newly elected in 1929. It was this Bill that caused the protective tariffs to be enacted in certain of Indian's export markets. The company was in a complete and total financial shambles and President Bauer resigned on June 7,

Right: *The first Indian Ace was simply an Ace with a pair of smaller diameter wheels and an Indian tank logo with a small Ace sub-script. For 1929 it became known as the Model 402 and came with the Indian leaf spring forks and brake.*

Indian

Indian
SCOUT

1929. Subsequent boards would consider entering the aeronautical and marine engine industries. Bauer was replaced by J. Russell Waite, who formulated a policy of supplying motorcycles to Indian dealers on a cash-with-order basis. This caused an outcry and saw some dealers resign their franchises, especially in view of the poor quality control being exercised on finished machines leaving Springfield.

E. Paul Du Pont acquired the company in 1930, as much for his interest in aviation as in motorcycles. Events within the world economy had taken a turn for the worse with the Wall Street, New York, Stock Exchange Crash of October 24, 1929. It was described by Variety, the theatrical trade paper, as 'Wall Street lays an Egg'. The crash finished Indian's involvement with aeroplanes and would lead directly to the Great Depression which lasted well into the 1930s.

Below: *The Indian Scout engine is reputed to have been one of Franklin's best designs and established the motorcycle as reliable. This is Roger Long's 1928 101 Scout outfit (left), bought secondhand in 1941 by his father, and which Roger has recently restored.*

Indian
SCOUT

1931 101 Scout

The 101 Scout was launched in 1928 to immediate critical acclaim. Many Indian dealers and riders thought that it was the finest motorcycle ever made. The 101 stayed in production until the end of 1931, the year that Ian Campbell's motorcycle (left) dates from. The 101 Scout was a redesigned Scout. Its wheelbase was lengthened and the seat was lowered. The frame was redesigned to give a more graceful shape and was complemented with a smaller fuel tank. The lengthened wheelbase contributed to the handling, for which the 101 Scout became legendary.

Specification

Model
101 Scout
Year
1931
Bore and stroke
2.875 × 3.5in.
Displacement
45cu. in. (740cc)
Bhp
20 (estimate)
Valve configuration
Side-valve
Top speed
70mph (112kph) (stock)
Fuel consumption
50mpg (estimate)
Transmission
Three-speed
Gearchange
Hand-shift
Wheelbase
57in.
Wheel diameter
18in.
Frame type
Rigid
Forks
Leaf sprung
Weight
370lb (168kg)

Indian
SCOUT

1931–1940

THE GLORY DAYS

MANY INDIAN riders felt that the 101 Scout was the finest motorcycle that the company had made and there was an outcry from both customers and dealers when it was discontinued in 1931. It was replaced for 1932 by a new Indian Scout that featured a 45cu. in. (740cc) engine in an Indian Chief frame and later in the same year the Scout Pony was added to the range. This second new machine was essentially a smaller displacement Scout, featuring as it did a 30.50cu. in. (500cc) V-twin engine. It utilized the cycle parts of a Prince single. The retail price of $225 made it the least expensive American V-twin motorcycle available, a very worthwhile selling point in a market adversely affected by the Great Depression.

Below and left: *Alan Forbes' Scout dates from 1931, the year when production of the 101 Scout was discontinued. It was powered by a 45cu. in. (740cc) engine.*

The handling characteristics of the new Scout were not up to those of the 101 models and some dealers resigned their franchises in frustration. From the factory's point of view, however, the new Scout was worthwhile because it reduced the number of different components they had to manufacture. It thereby made the process more cost effective which mattered in the dark days of the Depression.

Indian made a number of changes to the

design of their engines for 1933, of which undoubtedly the most important was the switch to dry sump lubrication on all their twin-cylinder engines. The dry sump system meant that oil would continuously circulate between the oil tank and engine so eliminating the need for the rider to hand-pump oil into the engine at specific intervals. This, in turn, reduced oil consumption. A 45cu. in. (740cc) variant of the Scout Pony – the Motoplane – was introduced in 1933 but the frame was not up to the increased power so the model was discontinued after less than 1000 had been made. It was in 1934 though that the new sports motorcycle would be manufactured in Springfield to properly supersede the 101 Scout.

The new machine was called the Sport Scout and was powered by a side-valve 42° V-twin engine that displaced 45.44cu. in. (747cc). Coil and battery ignition was the standard set-up although a magneto was available as an extra-cost option. The generator was positioned forward on the engine so the magneto was fitted on a bracket over the gearbox and driven by a chain and sprocket that engaged on the primary chain. It was a popular set-up for race bikes but it had problems with lubrication of the chain when used on the road for long distances and the timing could become inaccurate when the chain wore. The transmission was three-speed with a hand-shifter and foot-clutch. Girder forks and a bolt-together frame, named a 'keystone' frame by Indian, comprised the remainder of the motorcycle which rolled on 18in. diameter wheels. Overall the bike was aesthetically pleasing due in part to its short wheelbase of 56.5in and many American riders felt that it looked like a European bike. The Sport Scout was the motorcycle that would compete neck-and-neck with the 45cu. in. (740cc) Harleys on racetracks all over America and stay in production albeit gradually upgraded, until World War II changed things irrevocably. All Indian's Class C wins of this decade would be taken by riders aboard Sport Scouts. Rollie Free set a Class C speed record at Daytona Beach on a 1938 Sport Scout and tuned the Sport Scout model for riders such as 'Ironman' Ed Kretz. It is known that a showroom-stock Sport Scout could be expected to exceed 80mph (128kph) while a tuned one could be made to exceed 100mph (161kph). Many flat-track Sport Scouts were fitted with the smaller capacity Junior Scout tanks that carried all the fuel required for the duration of a race but also gave the impression of the hot-rod looking bike of the day. Jerry Hatfield, writing in *The Illustrated Indian Motorcycle Buyers' Guide*, summed up the appeal of the legendary Sport Scout thus:

> "The motor says let's get on with it and you begin to get the racer feel. You close your eyes to see more clearly. This is the 1938 Springfield mile and you're the world's greatest flat-tracker about to defeat the Harley gang. Eyes open again. In gear and away."

Spiegelhof, Kelly, Hill, James, Hillbish, Chasteen, Rodenburg and Kretz were the ones who actually did beat 'the Harley gang' for the decade and when they didn't beat them they most certainly gave them a run for their money.

Alongside the Sport Scout Indian kept the Standard Scout in production and renamed it the Scout 45 in 1936. The Dispatch-tow three-wheeler was fitted with a low compression version of the Sport Scout engine. The Indian Chief remained the larger capacity machine from Indian and it too was upgraded progressively through the decade. It had been introduced in 1922 and in 1932 a Chief with a taller profile was introduced. It had longer forks, a gas tank that covered the frame tubes and lubrication was total loss for the first year of sales. The famous World's Fair took place in 1939 and Indian displayed and marketed a range of motorcycles that featured more chrome plate than previously and an extravagant range of paint schemes reflecting Du Pont's ownership of the company. It was not until 1940 that the hugely valanced fenders that are synonymous with the Chief made their first appearance. They also appeared on the Scout models.

The roots of the famous four-cylinder

Right: *The Dispatch-tow, such as this one restored by Alan Forbes, was a three-wheeled machine offered by Indian from 1931 onward.*

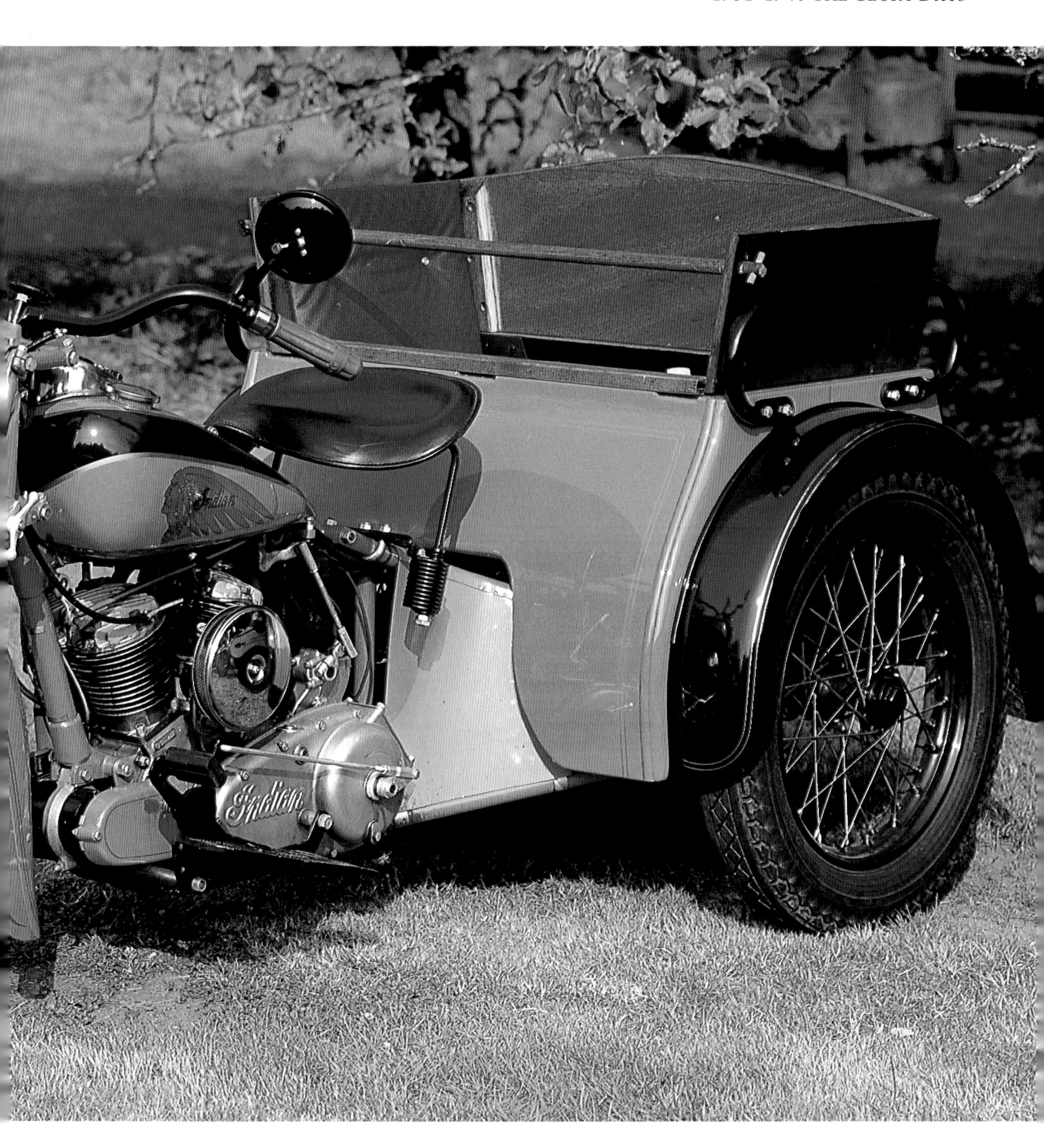
Indian
Indian

Above: *A Model 438. The designation refers to the engine type, a Four, and the year of manufacture, 1938. Its style contrasts with the earlier models: the 1931 Four of Alan Forbes (above right) and the 1934 Four of Jim Smith (below right).*

Indians are in the Depression. In 1927 Indian purchased the rights and tooling for the Ace motorcycle. This company had been set up by two Scottish brothers, Tom and Will Henderson, exponents of in-line four-cylinder machines. They had sold motorcycles in their own surname until this company was sold to Ignatz Schwinn who manufactured bicycles and owned Excelsior motorcycles. The brothers had worked for Schwinn but eventually left and started their own company again. It was known as Ace but when in 1922 one of the Henderson brothers, Will, was killed in an accident the company lost its way somewhat and changed hands more than once. Indian acquired it, no doubt realizing that the four-cylinder machines would complement their V-twin Chief models. Initially Indian did little to change the Fours beyond painting them Indian Red and renaming them the Indian Ace. More changes were made for 1929 and the motorcycle became known as the Indian Four Model 401. The Model 402 superseded the 401 and featured a five bearing crankshaft in the 77.21cu. in. (1265cc) engine. From then until 1941 the four-cylinder design was progressively upgraded in details. The only major change was short-lived. In 1936 Indian introduced what became somewhat derisively tagged as the 'upside-down' Indian. For whatever reason Indian's engineers had strayed from the proven inlet-over-exhaust design for an exhaust-over-inlet configuration. It was not a success for a number of reasons, not least of which was its cluttered appearance. The company persevered with the new design for 1937 but by 1938 had reverted to an inlet-over-exhaust type engine, with enclosed valve gear and automatic valve lubrication. While the Fours were expensive they often found favor with law enforcement agencies and the last batch manufactured before World War II were for one such customer.

Out at Muroc Dry Lake, California, the LA 45 Club held its annual speed trials sanctioned by the American Motorcyclist Association (AMA) and for 1936 they were held on Sunday, April 6. Fred Ludlow rode a 1936 Indian Sport Scout at 128.57mph (207kph) to win the 45cu. in. (740cc) flat-head class and Al Chasteen rode a 1935 Indian Chief at 125mph (201kph) to win the 74cu. in. (1200cc) flat-head class. In the overall results there were Indians in four of the top five places. The other machine, which came second at 126.76mph (204kph), was a Crocker. Al Crocker had formerly been the Los Angeles, California, distributor of Indians until he relinquished the franchise in order to manufacture the special performance eponymous machines.

Hap Jones was an extraordinary character whose involvement with motorcycling typifies motorcycle sport of the 1930s. At the age of 17 he rode his 1919 Indian machine from his home in Spokane, Washington, to San Francisco, California, where he found employment as a motorcycle messenger. Soon afterward he went to work repairing Harley–Davidsons at Dudley Perkins' dealership. It was while working here that he started racing, as several other mechanics in

Indian 4

Indian 4

the dealership were already doing. Perkins himself was a noted hillclimber. Hap Jones entered a number of local endurance races with some success but preferred hillclimbing and TT racing. The AMA had defined TT racing as being around a track that had both left and right turns to differentiate it from flat-track and dirt-track races and requiring at least one jump. Courses tended to be rough and in many ways the sport was a precursor of motocross. During the 1930s Jones traveled all over the western United States to compete in AMA national events on a JD model Harley–Davidson. It is reported that he very often frustrated official Harley–Davidson entrants by beating their newer VL models with his older JD. In 1936 Hap

Below and left: *The 1934 Chief – this one is owned by Jim Smith of New Jersey – was powered by a 42° V-twin engine of a side-valve configuration. The lubrication system was dry sump and the motor displaced 73.62cu. in. (1206cc).*

Jones won two races and was placed second in a third at Waco, Texas. He was awarded the Miniature TT Championship for his efforts. In 1938 Jones took his Indian Scout to Wichita, Kansas, to enter the Midwestern Championship. He took the title with wins in both time trials and TT events. He later planned to race at Daytona, Florida, and his entry for the 1942 running of the race had been accepted. However, the outbreak of World War II, following Pearl Harbor, forced its cancellation.

To support such competitive motorcycling efforts required an income. Jones ran a bicycle, and later a motorcycle, store through the Depression. He, his wife Rose and a single mechanic struggled in the economic climate of the time. Paying customers were welcome and desperate measures were required on occasions. In 1934 another

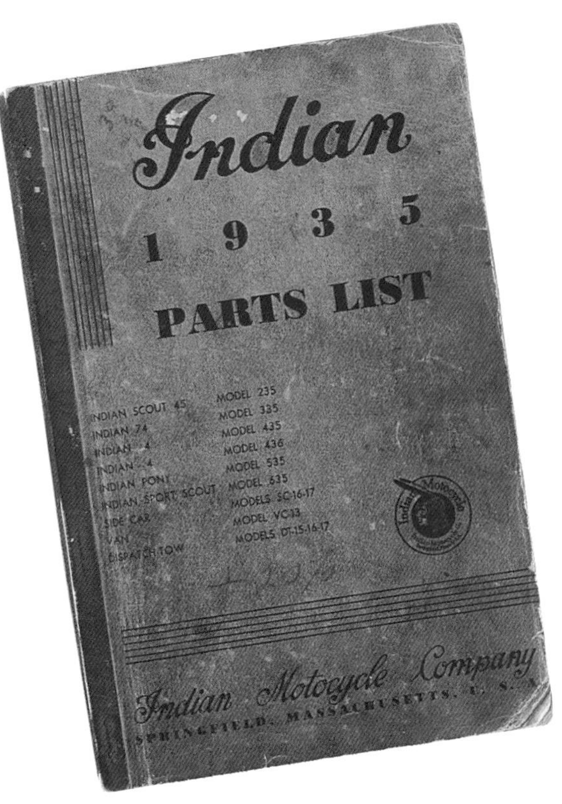

Above: *Indian dealers carried a full line of spare parts, as this catalog from 1933 shows. It included the Four, which had been introduced in 1928, although the short-lived 'upside-down' engine (left) in the Model 436 did not appear until 1936.*

motorcycle store was about to close and Hap Jones bought the inventory of spares. He did not have sufficient money to pay for the stock so simply took all the heaviest parts to a scrap dealer to raise the money in order to keep the remainder of the spares. He inaugurated a birthday party for friends and customers which grew into a large California Bay Area motorcycling event featuring hillclimbs and other competitions.

In 1936 Jones took over the San Francisco Indian franchise and business boomed until World War II intervened. He was turned down for military service for health reasons so spent the war years at his store. The vast majority of new machines were supplied to the military. By 1944 military demand had been all but satisfied and a shipment of 74cu. in. (1200cc) Indians was considered surplus to military requirements. Jones bought them with a borrowed $45,000. It was a wise move because he had sold them all within

three weeks. In the postwar years Jones started distributing parts nationally and he also began dealing in various imported makes of motorcycle as Indian went into decline. Later still he sold the dealership and took a privateer team of racers on Nortons to compete at Daytona in addition to sponsoring racers such as Dick Mann and races such as the San Jose Mile.

One of Indian's most legendary riders ever was Ed Kretz and one of the events that made him so was the first-ever Daytona 200 that was held in 1937 although his career had started earlier than this. Ed Kretz was born to parents of Swiss-German ancestry in San Diego, California, in 1911. He was the youngest of 11 children and after the family moved to Pomona, California, he took employment driving hay trucks through the Depression. In his early twenties he purchased an old VL Harley–Davidson from Floyd Clymer who was a Los Angeles, California, Indian franchisee. He went to watch a short-track race and became interested to the extent that he purchased a secondhand Rudge from Clymer in order to enter the events. Later he entered his VL in a speed event and finished second despite suffering a puncture and losing time as a result of it. Floyd Clymer was sufficiently impressed by the newcomer to arrange an Indian factory ride on a Sport Scout for future competitive events. Kretz went to work as a mechanic in Clymer's store during the week so he could race at weekends. In 1935 he entered the Ascot 100-miler (161km) and immediately took the lead. However, the Sport Scout was hampered by electrical problems said to have caused the ignition to short out against the saddle springs which meant that his bike coughed and spluttered its way around each lap. After six pitstops the fault was fixed and Kretz stepped up the pace. There were 43 laps of the race remaining and Kretz worked his way up the field from 19th to 6th. Despite not winning his potential was obvious.

Above: *Butch Baer on his 1937 Sport Scout in an American Historic Racing Motorcycle event at Daytona, Florida, in 1994. For 1937, on Chief models (right), the gear-shift was moved to the front of the gas tanks near the saddle, necessitating an extra linkage.*

The Depression had an adverse effect on motorcycle racing in the United States. Enthusiasts did not have money to spend traveling to race meets to either spectate or participate which caused fewer events to be promoted because of the sparse attendance. After the worst of the Depression had passed race fans and promoters again began to take an active interest in motorcycle racing and in the southeast of the United States a group came up with the idea of staging a big road-racing event. They revived an Atlanta, Georgia, event as a 200-miler (322km) run to the American Motorcyclist Association's new rules for Class C racing. This class was designed to revitalize motorcycle racing because it specified that to be eligible motorcycles should be street legal with only mufflers and lights removed. The maximum displacement which was permitted was 45cu. in.

(740cc), a figure probably arrived at as both the major United States domestic manufacturers – Indian and Harley–Davidson – offered a V-twin of this displacement.

The first of these 200-mile events was run in Savannah, Georgia, on April 26, 1932, and although there were as few as 14 machines entered the race went to a Harley–Davidson mounted rider, Ralph Edwards. The 1933 event, run on July 4, also went Harley's way when Bert Baisden took the first prize. For 1934 the event was moved to Jacksonville, Florida, and run earlier in the year. It attracted large crowds and the 1.5 mile (2.4km) circuit was fully paved in brick. A Harley–Davidson 45 ridden by Bremen Sykes once again took the honors for Milwaukee, although ironically-named Jesse James from Rhode Island brought his Indian 45 home in second place ahead of more than 30 other riders. In all, 68 riders started in the 1935 event and for much of the race the lead changed hands between Bill Carpenter on a Harley and Rody Rodenburg aboard a Sport Scout. In the last yards of the final lap Rodenburg edged past Carpenter, who was running out of gas, to break the Harley–Davidson domination of this southern 200-miler. This marathon event returned to Savannah, Georgia, for 1936 because of the growing crowds attending the race and the fact that the City of Savannah wanted the race back in their area simply because it was good for business. The 200-mile race held in these southern states was becoming prestigious and riders from all

Above: *Jim Smith of New Jersey owns this 1938 Indian Four. 1938 was the first year of 'paired' cylinders and the year Indian returned to the inlet-over-exhaust configuration after the 'upside-down' engine. The dash (left) had white gauges only in 1938.*

over the USA arrived for the fifth running of the event. Hap Alzina, the noted West Coast Indian distributor, brought two racers and race-prepared Indian Scouts to the event. Al Chasteen was one. He had won the Class C race in Oakland in San Francisco's industrial Bay Area the previous November. The other was a far less well-known 25-year-old newcomer: Ed Kretz. When the start flag dropped Kretz immediately went for the lead and clung to it until he had to pull in for gas. He regained the lead after refueling but three riders were close to him and he struggled to shake them off. One of these was his teammate Chasteen while the others were Babe Tancrede and Ralph Edwards. As the four headed for the checkered flag any one of them could have won but Kretz held off the challengers to finish first, Tancrede brought a 45 Harley in second while Chasteen edged ahead of Edwards to finish third. It was Ed Kretz's first major triumph and saw him win $400. However, it would not be his last big victory.

Above and right: *The Junior Scout featured a 30.50cu. in. (500cc) V-twin engine. It was always advertised with a woman rider and seen as a ladies' machine. This 1939 model is owned by Jon Mowen of Smithsburg, Maryland. The color is Navajo Blue.*

The City of Daytona Beach had allowed record-breaking runs to be made on the hard tidal sands of the Atlantic shore for many years and in 1937 invited the Southeastern Motorcycle Association to bring the 200-mile race to their area. The circuit would involve two straights, one along the beach and one along a surfaced road that ran parallel. The two straights were connected by sand turns making the total length 3.2 miles (5.1km). 63 laps were required to cover the total distance. As the race ran on both sand and pavement it would prove a testing combination for both the machines and their riders. The main event was the Class C race for almost showroom-stock motorcycles and in this class wins meant higher sales. A win at Daytona in the spring meant that the manufacturers of the victorious marque were able to trumpet their victory throughout the entire selling season. The Daytona 200 was about to become an institution that endures until the present time.

Ed Kretz was on the start line in a field that was in the main Harley–Davidson and Indian mounted although a number of Nortons were also entered. The race started in front of a crowd of some 15,000 spectators. When the flag dropped Kretz took his Sport Scout toward the front of the pack. By the end of the first lap he was in third place and leading by the end of the second. As the race went on Ed Kretz lapped the entire field of 85 other riders and convincingly won the first Daytona 200, his second 200-mile National Championship. Clark Trumbull from Washington, DC, was placed second on a Norton and a Florida resident, Ellis Pearce, finished third aboard a Harley–Davidson. Rody Rodenburg, who had won the 1935 event in Jacksonville, Florida, and also held the record for the 3005-mile (4836km) Los Angeles to New York City ride having accomplished it in 71 hours, finished seventh and Archie Sprague from Indiana and also on an Indian had placed fourth. The top 20 finishers consisted of seven Indians, eleven Harley–Davidsons and two Nortons. The new circuit only experienced one problem which was that of the incoming tide. Due to the start time of the race and the times of the tides, by the time that the racers were in the later laps the incoming tide was forcing them to take a longer line through the softer sand further up the beach or risk running through the edge of the water.

This problem was avoided for the 1938 running of the event simply by timing the start to coincide with the still ebbing tide rather than low water. Ed Kretz was back intent on defending his championship but crashed heavily in practice injuring the ligaments in his shoulder and spraining an ankle. Despite this he started the race along with 107 other riders and led for three laps but went out on lap 29 when his drive chain snapped. After this the lead was a battle between Lester Hillbish, an Indian rider from Pennsylvania, and two Harley riders,

Left: *For 1938 Indian returned to the proven inlet-over-exhaust configuration. Production of the Four was dropped in 1942 once a police contract (above right) was completed. Fours were expensive engines to manufacture (below right).*

STATE
POLICE

Ben Campanale and Tommy Hayes. In the end Campanale took the win only just ahead of Hillbish who was trailed by Hayes.

A much smaller field of riders started the 1939 event although there was considerable anticipation of a great dice for the win, primarily in view of the fact that both Kretz and Campanale were entered. It was also seen as a great Indian-v-Harley–Davidson showdown. Kretz charged into the lead from the start while 'Campy' was well down the pack but set about steadily working up toward the front. On lap seven he was in second place, a mere 10 seconds behind Kretz, and by lap nine Kretz's lead was less than six seconds. Disaster hit Kretz as the leaders went into lap 10. His Sport Scout caught fire and he lost four laps in containing the damage. Campanale looked set to win although Sam Arena, another famous Harley rider from California, challenged for the lead. He and Campanale passed and repassed each other for a number of laps until Arena crashed while negotiating one of the sand turns. His engine was damaged by the ingress of sand and he was forced to retire, leaving the way open for Campanale of the Rhode Island Ramblers MC to win his second successive Daytona 200. Kretz was eventually placed 25th but an Indian ridden by Bill Anderson finished third.

As the Daytona 200 was held in the spring it was becoming renowned as the first major motorcycle event of each year and so it was in 1940 for the fourth running of the Daytona 200. This race looked set to be a close run affair. Amongst others, Campanale, Tancrede and Arena were flying the flag for Harley–Davidson while Kretz and

Jimmy Kelly were doing the same for Indian. There were a total of 77 motorcycles at the start, of which only 15 finished. Kretz went out somewhere around the midway point because of mechanical problems as did the Harley riders, Campanale and Arena. The lead developed into a dice between Babe Tancrede and Jimmy Kelly, the latter having caught the leader on lap 57. With only six laps to go Kelly was challenging for a win but sadly his Indian developed mechanical problems forcing his retirement on lap 59. This left the race to go Harley's way although Wallace Aikens, a Florida resident, brought his Indian home in second place.

Left: *A 1940 Scout in race trim. Machines such as this upheld Indian's honor while competing with Harley's WRTT. The 45cu. in. (740cc) engine (above) could be tuned for speeds of over 100mph (161kph).*

Unfortunately for Jimmy Kelly history would almost repeat itself in the last Daytona 200 before World War II. Harley debuted their new 45cu. in. (740cc) Class C racer, the WRTT, while Indian riders still rode the proven Sport Scout. The Canadian Billy Mathews on a Norton was considered a strong contender and took the lead in the first lap but Armando Magri, a Californian on a WRTT, challenged strongly. Mathews crashed in the sand and Magri retired due to mechanical problems. This put Indian mounted Ted Edwards in the lead but he too had to retire with engine trouble. Jimmy Kelly then led the pack with Mathews coming back into contention after restarting following his crash. The race looked set to give Kelly the victory he had been denied the year before until mechanical problems forced his retirement, leaving the way open for the first foreign marque to win at Daytona.

In the postwar years Kretz again raced there on Indians and subsequently British motorcycles and led on many occasions but won only twice because of the failure of the machines. Kretz went on to become an Indian dealer in Monterey Park, a suburb of Los Angeles, California. After Indian's demise the dealership took on other franchises including that of BMW. He was a powerful stocky man and luckily survived a number of accidents during his racing career. Luck and skill were with him during the last big race before the outbreak of war, the 200-miler at Oakland, California. Kretz was well in the lead and coming up through the pack as he lapped the slower riders. A Texan, Tommy Hayes, in second place, increased the pace in an attempt to stop Kretz passing and pulled out to pass Ben Campanale but went into the north turn too fast and crashed. The crash brought Campanale off, Kretz nipped through between the riderless machines but the three racers following, John McCall, Jimmy Kelly and Sam Arena, were all brought down by one of the crashed bikes. Sam Arena laid his bike down at 100mph (161kph) and escaped serious injury. McCall and Hayes were killed, and Kelly and Campanale were hospitalized for almost a year. It was a bad day for motorcycle racing and reminiscent of the Newark, New Jersey, board-track crash in which Eddie Hasha and others had died 30 years earlier.

55
Indian

1940 Indian Dirt Tracker

Dean Nelson owns this prewar dirt-track racer, restored to its original specification and a high standard. Bikes that were regularly raced would look much more used than this because of damage done by dirt thrown up by the competing bikes. On race bikes such as these everything unnecessary was removed to make the machine as light in weight as possible. The pad on the rear fender was moved as close to the saddle as possible to allow the rider to move about and a front brake was not fitted in accordance with the rules. It was the immediate predecessor of bikes such as this that beat Harley–Davidson in two consecutive years in the late 1930s in the prestigious Langhorne, Pennsylvania, 100-mile National Championship.

Specification

Model
Indian Sport Scout
Year
1940
Bore and stroke
2.875 × 3.5in. (stock)
Displacement
45.44cu. in. (744.6cc) (stock)
Bhp
25 (stock)
Valve configuration
Side-valve
Top speed
85mph (137kph) (stock)
Fuel consumption
55mpg
Transmission
Three-speed
Gearchange
Hand-shift
Wheelbase
58in.
Wheel diameter
18in.
Frame type
Keystone
Forks
Girder
Weight
475lb (215.5kg) (stock)

Indian
Eighty

1941–1953

THE FINAL YEARS

THE JAPANESE airstrike against Pearl Harbor on Hawaii on December 7, 1941, jolted the American nation into World War II and within days the United States Marine Corps were fighting a desperate action to hold Wake Island, a tiny Pacific atoll up to that point used by Pan American Airways to refuel their four-engined flying boats for their around-the-globe services. The island assumed huge strategic importance in the coming struggle for domination of the Pacific. The Marines' stand for 16 days against overwhelming odds became the lead story on edition after edition of US newspapers. *The Washington Post* described it as "the stage for an epic in American military history, one of those gallant stands such as led Texans 105 years ago to cry 'Remember the Alamo'" It was also the first sign after the disaster at Pearl Harbor that although the road to victory would be long and costly, America, the most powerful industrial nation on earth, would ultimately win. The might of America's industry was about to be unleashed on the forces of the Rome–Berlin–Tokyo Axis. A part of the industry which would be included in this war effort were America's motorcycle manufacturers whose products were considered fundamental to making armies mobile.

In fact President Roosevelt had declared a limited emergency within a week of the beginning of the war in Europe which had started on September 1, 1939, with Germany's invasion of Poland. The President's action permitted further recruiting to both the US Army and the National Guard. The

Below: *Evelyn Erikson purchased this 1941 Sport Scout new in Miami, Florida, and still rides it today. The distinctive fenders (left) were retained on postwar Chiefs.*

process had started that summer when the strength of the army had been increased from 175,000 to 210,000 men. General Marshall, recently appointed Chief of Staff, established several tactical corps HQs with enough troops to create a fully functioning field army. He also reorganized the basic infantry divisions into five three-regiment 'triangular' divisions aimed at making them more maneuverable and flexible. In 1940 the first corps maneuvers since 1918 were held and in May these were followed by Corps-v-Corps exercises. While mechanization of the army had begun in 1936, it had been somewhat hampered by a lack of funds although both Indian and Harley–Davidson received contracts for 2000 motorcycles at a motorcycle reliability conference called by the Quartermaster Corps at Camp Holabird, Baltimore, in November 1938. Now in 1940 an amount of expenditure was permitted in order to purchase much-needed transport including motorcycles. The reason for this was that the reorganization intended that non-divisional cavalry in the form of cavalry recce squadrons would ride 'point' ahead of the new divisions. A squadron would consist of three recce troops and nine recce platoons that would be transported in a defined number of White Scout cars, Dodge Command cars and motorcycles, both solos and combinations. This promised to be a worthwhile business opportunity for the motorcycle manufacturers and three companies eventually supplied prototypes for testing, namely Indian, Harley–Davidson and Delco.

Indian were already part way through a military contract which they had received in October 1939 from the French Government. It was for 5000 Indian Chiefs, with sidecars, in a militarized form. The scale of the contract was likely to cause a number of production difficulties for Indian who were still struggling out of the Depression so it was decided to produce the motorcycles for this contract in two batches of 2500 machines, and during January and February 1940

Left: *The US Government specified its requirements for military motorcycles including standardized parts such as these twin tail-lights and, of course, drab olive paint. Many civilian parts, such as the dashboard (below), were used with this finish.*

extra workers were taken on at the factory. The early months of 1940 were desperate times in war-torn Europe and some 2200 crated Indians were loaded aboard the *SS Hanseatic Star* which sailed from New York for Le Havre, France, on April 12, 1940. The ship was a victim of the German U-boats operating in the North Atlantic and was lost to a torpedo. Whether or not the motorcycles would have been much use to the French war effort anyway is debatable as by June 1940 the British were evacuating their army from the beaches at Dunkirk, France having fallen to the Axis. The motorcycles built for the French Army were designated the 340-B, displaced 74cu. in. (1200cc), and were derived from the Indian Chief. Subsequently the machine was supplied for service in other Allied armed forces and US domestic law enforcement agencies.

The machine that Indian supplied to the US Army for evaluation was initially designated the 640 Model. It was assembled from a combination of existing components from Indian's Junior and Sport Scout models. The new military model was fitted with an engine based on the 30.50cu. in. (500cc) unit from the Junior Scout but with a lower compression ratio, mild valve timing and modifications to ensure reliability in military service. Transmission was a standard Chief gearbox and a standard enclosed chain drive primary drive. Final drive was by chain. Much of the remainder of the machine was Sport Scout including the two-piece frame, while the fork legs were similar but longer to increase ground clearance. The front and rear fenders were not valanced like the civilian type and allowed substantial clearance above the tires to reduce the likelihood of their becoming clogged with mud in difficult conditions. Certain military components were fitted including a heavy duty rear rack on which saddlebags were mounted, military blackout lights, and an Oakes oil-bath airfilter to maintain engine longevity in dusty conditions.

The staff of the Mechanized Cavalry Board at Fort Knox, Kentucky, undertook

Right: *The 640-A engine was based on that of the prewar Junior Scout. It too displaced 30.50cu. in. (500cc) but had a lower compression ratio and milder valve timing.*

the testing of motorcycles for the US Army. Elsewhere other machines were being tested; at Fort Benning, Georgia, for example, Indian and Delco trikes were being tested. (This project led to considerable work by the three manufacturers including the production of prototypes and debate as to whether they should be chain or shaft driven but ultimately it all led nowhere.) Much of the testing at Fort Knox was done at low speeds in order to gauge the running temperatures of engines to assess their suitability for convoy escort duties and cross-country work although the machines were expected to be capable of 65mph (104kph). The testers liked certain aspects of each manufacturer's machine and disliked others. The left-hand throttle fitted to Indians was praised as it allowed riders to use their right hand for traffic signaling during convoy duties. The Harley–Davidson WL model was perceived as more rugged but the Delco machine, the design of which was based closely on a BMW, was praised for its shaft drive, tele-

scopic forks, considerable ground clearance and light weight. This would lead to further development work by both Harley and Indian resulting in the XA and 841 models respectively. However, before this came the 640-B which was a 45cu. in. (740cc) version of the 640 which was referred to as the 640-A. The 640-B was subsequently redesignated the 741 and it was preferred for US conditions because of its higher performance. Both models were accepted by the US testers and an open-ended contract allowed the company to commence production of them. A further open-ended contract was awarded in January 1941 and almost 11,000 machines rolled off the Springfield lines in that year

Below: *Robin Markey of Bob's Indian Sales of Etters, Pennsylvania, seen here with his restored military Indians – a 1943 Model 741-B on the left and a 1940 640-A on the right. The main difference between the two is the engine capacity: the 640-A displaced 30.50cu. in. (500cc) while the 741-B displaced 45cu. in. (740cc).*

Left: *'Essential Use' bikes, such as this 1945 model belonging to Jamie Seidell, were the only new bikes supplied, other than official models, during the war years. Steve Teddaton's 841 (above) was an experimental V-twin built at the request of the US Army.*

which was the highest production figure since the boom of the early 1920s.

Late in 1941 Indian received an order for 5000 640-A models from Great Britain which, at that time, was reeling under the onslaught of the German Luftwaffe. Aerial bombing had destroyed much of the country's industrial capacity including the famous Triumph works in Coventry, England. The 640-A model was chosen by the British because of a greater fuel economy than the larger capacity 741. Production of both 640-A and 741 models continued through 1942 and a smaller number of Indian Chiefs were also being produced for law enforcement agency contracts and 'Essential Use' customers. This latter category was the only way individuals could purchase a new motorcycle during the war years and to qualify they had to prove that the machine was necessary for their duties in relation to the United States' war effort. Essential Use motorcycles were supplied to the most basic specification and with a minimum of chrome plate. All civilian vehicle production across the United States was halted on February 9, 1942. Indian did however continue to advertise their products, no doubt anticipating a postwar demand for new machines. One such advert showed a group of riders taking cover alongside their Indian motorcycles. It read: 'In a militant world "Indians" Scout ahead'.

In August 1943 Indian received an Army–Navy Production Award generally known as the 'E for Excellence' Award. A ceremony was held in the grounds of the Indian factory at which an Army–Navy 'E' pennant was hoisted to the top of the flagpole, having been presented by Brigadier General Burton O. Lewis, chief of the Boston, Massachusetts, Ordnance District. Dwight L. Moody, Indian's Vice-President, made an acceptance speech and President E. Paul Du Pont expressed his appreciation to the employees. 'E' pins were presented to the employees by a retired naval officer, William M. Saunders, and a speech of acceptance was made by John A. Bible, President of the Indian Employees' Association, who had worked for the company for 31 years. An estimated 9000 Lend–Lease machines were supplied to the Russian Red Army and were among the total of 42,044 machines made during the war years.

The 841 was the result of the US Army's fascination with shaft drive motorcycles. The German Army motorcycle combinations featured shaft final drive and horizontally-opposed engines, two things that were seen as advantages over chain drive V-twins because of their minimal maintenance requirements. Shaft drive did away with the need for continual chain adjustments and flat-twins ran at lower temperatures meaning that the engine had a greater life between rebuilds. Both Harley–Davidson and Indian were persuaded to bid for motorcycle contracts that specified these features. Indian supplied the 841 which featured a transversely-mounted 45cu. in. (740cc) V-twin engine and shaft drive to the rear hub. As with their other military machines the company used existing components wherever possible including a number of Sport Scout engine parts. Suspension was plunger at the rear, a girder fork set-up was new from Indian, and the handlebars were rubber mounted to reduce the vibration felt by the rider. The 841 was Indian's first foot-shift motorcycle. In the relatively low state of tune as suitable for military purposes it was still capable of 70mph (112kph). The army ordered 1000 of the new machine to be supplied for evaluation and ordered 1000 of the competing Harley–Davidson XA that also featured plunger rear suspension and shaft drive. It differed in that the engine was a flat-twin and the forks were telescopic.

The army deferred its decision on which model to order in larger numbers until into 1943 when it anticipated that all of the initial batches would have been supplied. They also suggested that whichever would be chosen would be manufactured by both companies in the way Willys Jeeps were being manufactured by Ford. Mention of the Willys Jeep here is not as irrelevant as it might seem because the Jeep was to have significant impact on the army's requirements for motorcycles. The light four-wheel drive Willys Jeep became a mass-produced reality in 1941 and soon relegated the motorcycle to a rear echelon service role because the Jeep was more suited to combat applications and for carrying fighting men and their equipment across rough terrain. As a result of this neither the Harley XA or the Indian 841 were ever ordered in great numbers. The Jeep also sounded the death knell for the various trike projects under consideration.

Below: *Canada came to Britain's aid in World War II and its army were amongst Indian's customers for motorcycles as this Dutch enthusiast's restored machine shows.*

Of the 1056 841s produced some were distributed to army installations and many remained in Springfield, Massachusetts, at the factory until they could be sold as army surplus in 1944. As the tides of war turned in favor of the Allies in both the Pacific and European theaters of operations other batches of motorcycles became available for sale to the public including 4600 offered for sale in spring 1944. Of these 1900 were Indians. Another batch of 1500 Indians from 3500 motorcycles was offered that August. Military contracts began to be cancelled although Indian received contracts for

Right: *America's entry into World War II meant the suspension of civilian motorcycle manufacture, although parts were still supplied. The only new Indians were military models. This restored example (below) is authentic down to a GI's equipment.*

the manufacture of naval ordnance and continued making spares for its military motorcycles. The US Government later declined to pay for these parts which left Indian once again in a precarious financial position because the losses incurred absorbed all the company's money intended for postwar development of their range.

The career of Francis 'Cliff' Clifford gives an indication of what the immediate postwar motorcycling scene was like. He started working with motorcycles in the late 1930s when he took a job as a motorcycle messenger for a photographer. Business was sufficiently good for him to be able to buy a new Indian Scout in 1939. He intended to start motorcycle racing in 1940 and entered a Triumph Tiger 100 machine in a race at a San Francisco track. While dicing with one of Dudley Perkins' riders, Cottrell, on a WR Harley–Davidson he crashed into the trackside fencing and broke a leg. By the time he had recovered from his injury World War II had commenced and racing had been suspended as a result of tire and fuel rationing. In 1947 Cliff was out racing on a 101 Indian Scout that he taken in trade for his Triumph and started work for Hap Jones at his Indian dealership. Cliff fitted Bonneville camshafts and other tuning parts into his engine and enjoyed a very popular period of motorcycle racing. Each weekend there were race events at circuits in San Francisco, Davis, Stockton, Tulare, Sacramento, Lodi and Belmont. At the latter track there were as many as 200 races per year. Later Clifford had a spell working for Dudley Perkins on that dealer's Harley WR racers and spent time on the road with the team working on the bikes between races. He was not paid a salary for this and earned a living from winnings from amateur races. He quit racing in 1953 and returned to work for Hap Jones.

The famous Daytona 200 race had been suspended for the duration of World War II

Indian 4

Indian 4

the dealership were already doing. Perkins himself was a noted hillclimber. Hap Jones entered a number of local endurance races with some success but preferred hillclimbing and TT racing. The AMA had defined TT racing as being around a track that had both left and right turns to differentiate it from flat-track and dirt-track races and requiring at least one jump. Courses tended to be rough and in many ways the sport was a precursor of motocross. During the 1930s Jones traveled all over the western United States to compete in AMA national events on a JD model Harley–Davidson. It is reported that he very often frustrated official Harley–Davidson entrants by beating their newer VL models with his older JD. In 1936 Hap

Below and left: *The 1934 Chief – this one is owned by Jim Smith of New Jersey – was powered by a 42° V-twin engine of a side-valve configuration. The lubrication system was dry sump and the motor displaced 73.62cu. in. (1206cc).*

and the first postwar running was in 1947. Motorcycle race fans flocked to the Florida resort in record numbers: an estimated 27,500 people arrived to see the 142 entered riders vying for the $1000 prize money. An unusual occurrence during this race was a brush fire alongside the track which was not severe enough to stop the racing although gusting winds meant that the riders were at times passing through the flames. The fourth place finisher Bob Stuth (Harley–Davidson) had a burned and blistered hand. The battle for the lead was where most attention was turned, however. Ed Kretz riding a Norton and Floyd Emde riding a Harley were dicing

Above: *The postwar Indian Chief was a truly magnificent motorcycle as evidenced by the Seidell family's outfit, and by this red Chief (below and left). Model 841 design girder forks were used from 1947 as was the illuminated Indian head fender light.*

for the lead ahead of Johnny Spiegelhof on an Indian Scout wearing race number 2 and sponsored by Krause Indian Sales. Emde's Harley suffered a breakdown on lap 6 and Kretz went out with chain problems during lap 12, leaving Spiegelhof in the lead. Bobby Hill, an Indian rider from Ohio, fought his way up through the pack to second place by lap 20. However, brake problems forced him out of the running. Spiegelhof from Milwaukee, Wisconsin, eventually gave Indian its second Daytona 200 win trailed by Ted Edwards from Atlanta, Georgia, also on an Indian Scout. Third went to Alli Quattrochi, a Rhode Islander, on a Harley–Davidson.

The racers came back to Daytona in the spring of 1948 for the second postwar running of the race which was scheduled to take place on a new 4.1 mile (6.6km) racetrack. This had been necessitated by the recent construction of houses on the site of the original racetrack on the Daytona peninsula. Both Indian's former winners, Kretz and

Spiegelhof, were entered as were other winners including Harley riders Ben Campanale and Babe Tancrede as well as Norton rider Billy Mathews. Floyd Emde from San Diego, California, had entered on one of only 50 special Indian Sport Scouts that had been built for racing. These Sport Scouts were designated the Model 648 and were all assembled by a three-man team led by Jimmy Hill who were employed in Indian's experimental department. They utilized the longer 741 forks and 841 cylinders. The engines featured narrower flywheels which were machined from cast steel and graduated diameter oilways in the crankshaft assembly. Through modification of the front camshaft the 1948 Chief oil pump was incorporated and drove a vertically-mounted magneto. To fit this several cooling fins had to be trimmed. Larger domed pistons were used to raise the compression ratio and required the reshaping of the combustion chambers. The 648s are generally referred to as 'Big Base' Scouts because of the large sump cast into the rear of the crankcases. It has been suggested that Spiegelhof's 1947 Daytona-winning motorcycle was a prototype Big Base. Emde's 648 was sponsored by Guy Urquhart, a San Diego dealer, and after the race started he led it from start to finish, the first Daytona winner to do so. As well as legends like Ed Kretz and Cannonball Baker who were there to see him at the finish so were Noel MacIntyre, Emde's mechanic, and the new Company President, Ralph B.

Below: *Indian promoted their Models 149 and 249 for 1949. The 149 (above right) was a single, while the 249 (below right) was a twin, such as this one owned by Dennis Bolduc. Sadly, these bikes were not entirely reliable so spare parts were often needed (left).*

Indian

Indian

Indian

Rogers. Although Emde had led from start to finish the race was close. Canadian Billy Mathews on a Norton stayed with the leader until the mid-point of the race when he had problems which delayed him while refueling. Once he was back on the track he was a minute behind Emde but rode hard to make up the deficit and the race remained undecided into the last laps. The 1949 event saw Nortons take the top three places and indicated changing times for the US domestic manufacturers.

In March 1945 newspapers announced that President Du Pont had been elected Chairman of the Board at Indian. Du Pont was in poor health and it was thought that he did not feel confident enough about the future to face Indian's problems so he agreed to sell the company. In October it was finally purchased by Ralph Buron Rogers, an industrialist and millionaire. He owned and had interests in a variety of industrial concerns including diesel engine manufacturers, lawnmower producers and railway car manufacturers. Later Rogers also acquired the Torque Engineering Company who were planning to produce lightweight motorcycles at Plainville, New Jersey. Although not a motorcyclist Rogers set out to assess the state of the companies he had purchased and learned to ride a motorcycle. He and several others in positions of authority were coming to a similar conclusion about the future market in the USA. They felt that there was likely to be a demand for small, cheap, lightweight motorcycles but that many dealers would need to change their approach to sell-

Left: *A 1947 Chief with a period custom Rainbow paint scheme in the popular red and yellow colors. Cream (below) was also a stock Chief color as this 1953 rear fender shows. An ex-police bike, it belongs to Earl Supernant of Chicopee, Massachusetts.*

ing. They would have to become more progressive and smarten up their dealerships. Rogers thought that marketing a line of Torque lightweights alongside the traditional Indian products would once again make the company prosperous. The Torque lightweights were a single of 11cu. in. (180cc), a twin of 22cu. in. (360cc) and a four of 44cu. in. (720cc) assembled with interchangeable components.

This plan went ahead although postwar inflation and the Marshall Plan, aimed at helping Europe's economic recovery, made the years following World War II trying ones for domestic manufacturers. The establishing of the production of the Torque lightweights put considerable demands on the company and required a reorganization in Springfield. While the project was being evaluated and costed, Indian Chiefs were produced and started rolling off the line in 1946. They featured girder forks of the same design that had featured on the experimental 841. Some dealers were reassured by this but others demanded the return of the prewar Sport Scout which they felt was at least partially responsible for Indian's reputation because of its race-winning successes. The war though had changed things in a way from which there was no turning back. The British bike invasion was coming despite Indian wins in the first postwar races such as the Five Star race at the Wisconsin State Fair. At this event Indian riders, including the late great Bobby Baer, won both the amateur and expert 5-milers and the expert 15-miler. It was the 1948 Daytona 200 though that was to be Indian's last great ride.

The Torque lightweights were not to be a success because the cost estimates for their production were so far under the real costs and caused an increase in prices almost immediately after the machines went on sale. Once again Indian were in a difficult financial position. Behind the scenes financial dealing and merging of companies was going on and to compound the situation there were numerous reliability problems with the Torque models. In what was rapidly becoming a sad state of affairs a number of dealers including well-known ones such as Guy Urquhart, Hap Jones, Hap Alzina and Ed Kretz held a meeting. The upshot of this was that Kretz went to the factory to test the Torque machines and advise the management about them. The financial situation worsened. One bank in particular began to foreclose on the debt it was owed while the engineers sought to rectify the faults common in the Torque models. Rogers travelled to England to meet with John Brockhouse, Managing Director of Brockhouse Engineering Ltd of Southport, England. It was not strictly the end but Indian's proud history was essentially over. The company stayed in business importing British bikes.

It also experimented with a Vincent–HRD powered Indian Chief as a backdoor route to modernizing the Chief line. The Warrior was brought out in view of the failure of the Torque design. It was a 30.50cu. in. (500cc) vertical-twin of decidedly European appearance. The final blow to Indian's chance of survival came from something completely unrelated to motorcycles: the British Government devalued its currency, the pound, almost 20 percent. This had the effect of drastically reducing the price of their exported motorcycles, meaning that

Left: *While the Indian Verticals were of a decidedly European appearance, they made much of their Indian connections. The 1950 TT Warrior (below) belongs to Chris Lord from New York. The 1951 Warrior (right) belongs to Joey Bollenbach of East Dundee, Illinois. Both are based on the same 30.50cu. in. (500cc) vertical parallel twin engine.*

Indian were unable to compete on price. Considerable wrangling had been going on at management level but regardless of the rights and wrongs the outcome was that the banks gained control of Indian and divided it into two companies. One would be known as the Indian Sales Corporation which would distribute numerous British brands in the USA, while a subsidiary of the Atlas Corporation – the Titeflex Corporation – would continue the manufacture of Indian Chiefs. These continued to be made until 1953. In that year Titeflex closed down the motorcycle production operation as a result of it making insufficient profits. It was an ignominious end for a company that through its history had a reputation for innovation and engineering excellence.

1941 Indian Four

The Indian Four motorcycle reached its peak in terms of both engineering development and opulence in the last year before America's involvement in World War II. Production of non-essential civilian machines was stopped after the Japanese attack on Pearl Harbor. After the cessation of hostilities the Fours were not reintroduced by Indian because of high manufacturing costs and the disappointingly small volume of sales.

Specification

Model
Indian Four
Year
1941
Bore and stroke
2.76 × 3.25in.
Displacement
77.21cu. in. (1265cc)
Bhp
40
Valve configuration
Overhead-inlet
Side-exhaust
Top speed
80mph (120kph)
Fuel consumption
50mpg
Transmission
Three-speed
Gearchange
Hand-change
Wheelbase
62in.
Wheel diameter
18in.
Frame type
Plunger
Forks
Leaf sprung
Weight
568lb (257kg)

Indian

TOWARD THE FUTURE

WHILE THE ENDING of the manufacture of Indian Chiefs was the end of the Springfield-produced Indians it wasn't quite the final curtain for the Indian brand or indeed the marque as a whole. The brand did not die because of the efforts of an organization called the Indian Sales Corporation and the marque has not died because of the efforts of Indian enthusiasts worldwide.

The Indian Sales Corporation specialized in selling a number of imported makes of British bikes. This corporation retailed AJS, Douglas, Excelsior, Matchless, Norton, Royal Enfield and Vincent. They also sold various motorcycles that were simply other makes rebadged as Indians. The 1951-53 Indian Brave was in fact a side-valve single built in England by Brockhouse, the company which had gained control of Indian. This Brave displaced 15cu. in. (248cc), was capable of 68mph (109kph) and returned 82mpg, according to *Cycle* magazine's road-test of July 1952. It featured an Albion gearbox, Lucas electrics, Smiths speedo, Lycette saddle and Amal carburetor, which were all proprietary English parts. However, the Brave did not sell in very great numbers and for the year of 1954 the company sold Corgi folding motorcycles, which were assembled by Brockhouse, and Royal Enfield machines. For 1955 these latter motorcycles were rebadged as Indians and featured what were considered appropriate names such as Fire Arrow, Tomahawk, Trailblazer and Woodsman. These machines were respectively the Royal Enfield Clipper, Meteor Minor, Meteor 700, and an off-road version of the

Left: *Lee 'Pops' Standley built the engine for The Shop's vintage dirt-track racing Indian. Neil Grieve, of Edinburgh, Scotland, rebuilt this 1947 Indian Chief (below).*

Bullet. The company played down its heritage and introduced a Chief for the 1959 sales year but in reality it was simply a Trailblazer, or Enfield Meteor 700, fitted with 16in. diameter wheels and 5.00 × 16 tires and a few other minor styling changes.

AMC – Associated Motorcycles – of Great Britain, manufacturers of Matchless and AJS machines, acquired the rights to the name in 1960 and renamed dealerships AMC/Indian. They did not rebadge their bikes as Indians but merely marketed them through the established dealer network. In 1963 the Berliner Motor Corporation took over the distribution of AMC bikes and dropped the name Indian. It resurfaced in 1967 when Floyd Clymer, a character who had a lifetime of involvement with Indian, sought to produce a new model. Clymer was born in 1895 and had started racing on a Harley–Davidson around the age of 21. He became the Denver, Colorado, Harley–Davidson dealer and held the franchise until 1918. In the early 1920s he rode a stripped-down Scout to the top of Pike's Peak in Colorado. He disproved the sceptics who said it was impossible by getting further than any of the previous attempts. This generated a great deal of publicity and no doubt assisted Clymer when he took on the Indian franchise in Denver, Colorado. By 1925 he had diversified into the manufacture and marketing of a car spotlight, allowing the motorcycle sales side of his business to decline, so the factory passed the Indian franchise on to Dick Richards.

Above: *The 15.25cu. in. (250cc) Indian Brave of the early 1950s was actually manufactured in England by the Brockhouse Company. This 1944 Chief outfit (right) was rescued from Peru, South America, by California-based Indian specialist Mike Tomas and restored to running condition.*

Richards was loyal to Indian and a champion of lightweight motorcycles such as the Prince. He owned one himself and entered it in local motorcycling events. Competition between motorcycle dealers was keen and the Harley dealer was now Walter Whiting. Richards and Whiting worked together in friendly rivalry promoting motorcycling in general, thereby generating increased sales. Floyd Clymer sought to regain a motorcycle sales franchise and is alleged to have pulled strings behind the scenes to regain the Denver Harley–Davidson franchise. This he achieved in the spring of 1929 through the appointment of one of his own employees, H.D. Cooper, to the position of franchisee. Whiting went to work for Richards taking his former sales manager with him but formidable competition from Cooper and Clymer, the worsening relationship Indian dealers were having with the Indian factory, and the onset of the Depression forced the Richards dealership into bankruptcy.

As Indian's downward spiral of decline became more and more rapid Hap Alzina, a West Coast distributor, and Floyd Clymer attempted to purchase Indian's remaining assets from Brockhouse Ltd in England. The English company did not answer his com-

munications which led Clymer to write to *Cycle* magazine in May 1954 accusing the British company of deliberately ruining Indian. By the mid-1960s Clymer was still persevering with dreams of new Indians and had begun working with Friedel Munch, the German who had designed the Mammoth, a NSU car engined motorcycle. Munch was to design a derivative of the Mammoth that was fitted with a Indian Sport Scout V-twin engine. The prototype was exhibited at the Anaheim, California, Motorcycle Show in late 1967 but never went into production. It is thought that the retail price would have been too high to attract volume sales. The bike was a slightly odd-looking machine, being something of an uncomfortable mix of contemporary European café-racer styling and old-fashioned Indian V-twin engine. Next, Floyd Clymer used the Indian script-logo on the gas tanks of minibikes. These were the 3.05cu. in. (50cc) Jawa CZ two-stroke and the 3.05cu. in. (50cc) Italian Minarelli. The minibikes were relatively successful, in terms of sales, unlike a number of Velocette, Norton and Horex engined bikes. Floyd Clymer died in 1970.

Above: *Kiwi Indian Parts in Riverside, California, and The Shop, in Ventura, California, run by David Hansen (right). The photographs indicate how many Indians there are still left to restore, as well as how much ephemera there is to collect (left).*

In the same year, 1970, the Indian brand was removed even further from its roots when a Californian lawyer purchased the name to use on a range of Taiwanese minibikes. This concern was based in Gardena, California, and opened a factory in Taiwan. It is reported to have manufactured 20,000 minibikes in 1973 but was declared bankrupt in 1976. At this time the company was based in Culver City, California, and produced the MI 175. This model was powered by a two-stroke single-cylinder engine which was of 10.43cu. in. (171cc) displacement through a bore and stroke of 66 × 50mm. It had a compression ratio of 9:1 and was fitted with a Mikuni carburetor. The engine

Indian
MOTORCYCLES
Indian

developed 17bhp at 7000rpm and transmission was five-speed, giving a top speed of 70mph (112kph). It was kick-started. The MI 175 was in all respects a completely conventional lightweight trailbike of its time with telescopic front forks and a rear swinging arm, drum brakes and six volt electrics. Some MI 175 motorcycles were exported and there were concessionaires in overseas countries including K.I. Andrews Ltd of Greenwich, London, in England. Later a four-stroke lightweight was manufactured and sold as the 'Indian Four', a far cry indeed from the elegant and opulent four-cylinder machines of prewar days. Another early 1970s attempt to manufacture Indians was made by a Springfield industrialist, Charles Manthos, who was also a longtime Indian enthusiast. He planned an updated engine and transmission that could be retro-fitted into later Chiefs and Blackhawk models. High tooling costs were just one of the obstacles faced by this operation.

Harry V. Sucher, writing in *The Iron Redskin* in 1977, commented on the uncertainties of the legal ownership of the trademark 'Indian'. Then, in 1989, Jerry Hatfield commented in *The Illustrated Indian Motorcycle Buyer's Guide* that he 'wouldn't be surprised if the revered old name shows up again on some two-wheeler far removed from the true Indian story'. Both these remarks were prophetic as in the early 1990s there were at least two attempts to revive the Indian marque once again. At least two companies sought to produce a heavyweight cruiser-type motorcycle. They were possibly spurred on by Harley–Davidson's late 1980s and early 1990s success in this market. One concern was headed by Philip S. Zanghi and known as Indian Motorcycle Inc. The company manufactured Indian-branded clothing in order to finance production of a limited run of motorcycles which were referred to as Indian Chiefs. He based himself in Springfield, Massachusetts, in an attempt to further the Indian connection. Meanwhile, elsewhere in the United States, in Albuquerque, New Mexico, a company calling itself Indian Motorcycle Manufacturing Inc also planned to relaunch a motorcycle called the Indian Chief. The existence of two companies with the same idea led to considerable litigation concerning ownership of the various trademarks including the very name Indian itself. Zanghi planned to produce a motorcycle with Indian's classic full-fendered lines and a 92cu. in. (1511cc) 60° V-twin engine that featured three valves per cylinder and was liquid-cooled. The frame

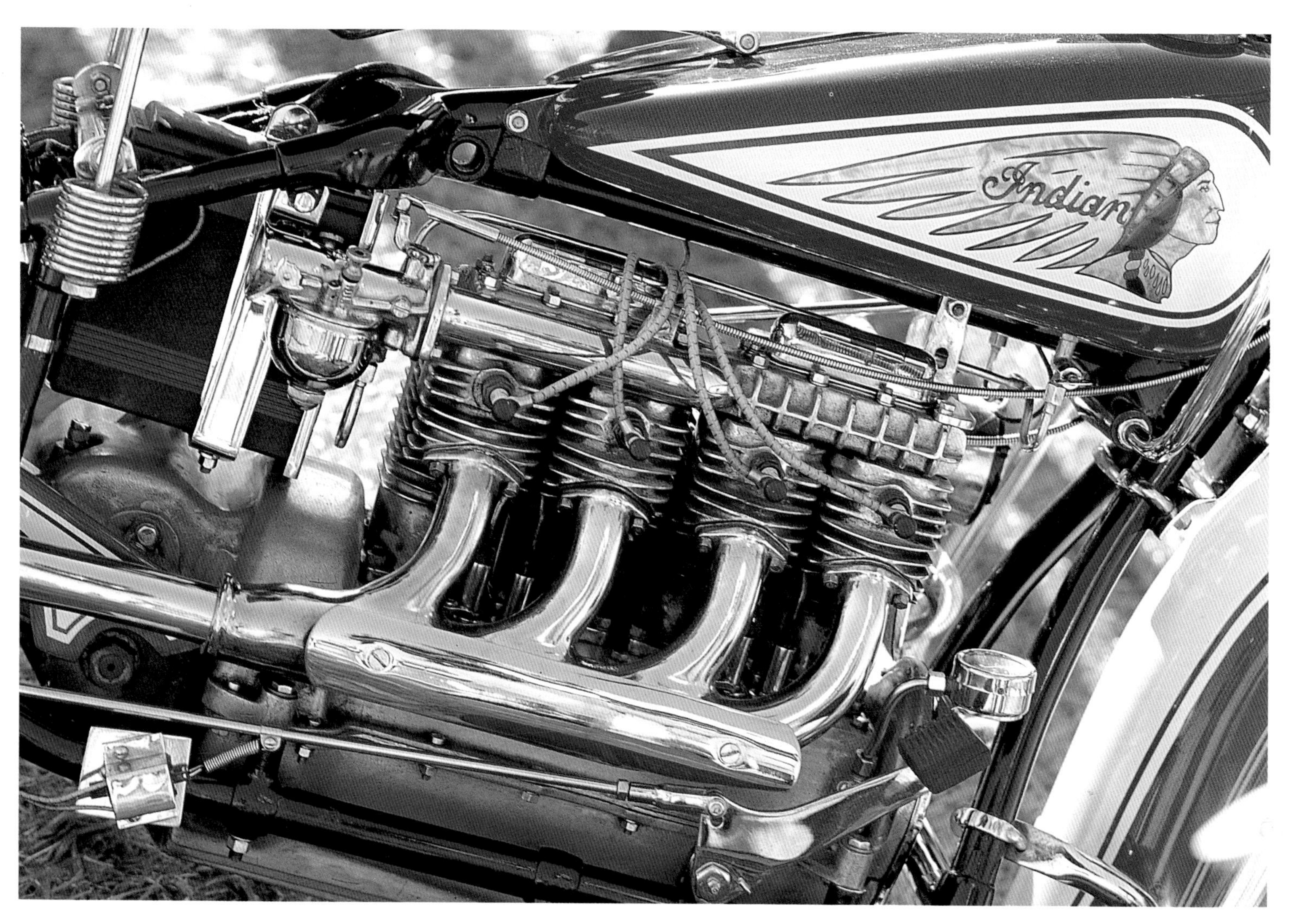

Left: *Old motorcycles often require considerable restoration. This machine was assembled by Tony Leenes from used parts. Early Indian Fours (right) required frequent manual valve lubricaton while this was done automatically on later models (above).*

would incorporate an aluminum swingarm as part of its design which intended to update the Chief.

Wayne Baughman's motorcycle known as the IMMI Century Chief has been displayed in prototype form. Like its potential competitor, the machine keeps the full-fendered lines of a real Indian Chief but seeks to update them. The motive power for the Century Chief is a V-twin engine designed and manufactured by Cyril Batten of the Batten Corporation. The design of the machine was a liquid-cooled V-twin of

100.6cu. in. (1680cc) displacement through bore and stroke both of four inches. The design featured three valves per cylinder, two oil pumps (one for cooling and one for lubrication) and a pressure-fed crankshaft. Fuel injection is another up-to-date touch as is a five-speed transmission. More latterly there has been yet another attempt to relaunch the Indian brand by an Australian named Mauritz Heyim-Langridge who was involved with the import of motorcycles into Australia. He anticipated building a motorcycle to be called an Indian that would be powered by an engine designed by John Britten, who had success with race bikes with engines of his own design. Unfortunately, John Britten passed away before the project saw fruition. The thing all these attempts have in common, apart from failure, is that the only connection with the real Indians – those from the Springfield factories – is that they seek to use the same legendary name because of its place in motorcycling history. They might just as well have chosen other brand names.

The other aspect of Indians post-1953 has been the growing numbers of enthusiasts

that they have attracted. There were long-standing Indian enthusiasts while the bikes were still being manufactured so it followed that many would remain interested in the Springfield machines after the demise of the original company. Add this to the fact that old motorcycles of every make and size became collectable with the growth of interest in so-called 'classic' bikes and a mas-

Left: *Interest in old Indians is worldwide. Here, participants in the European Indian Rally in Scotland sedately tour the Highlands while (above) the racing team, with Doc Battsleer (kneeling), from Daytona Beach, Florida, make their Indians run to top speed.*

sive explosion of interest in American-made motorcycles generally. Considering Harley–Davidson's phenomenal success it was also inevitable that Indians would be seen as equally desirable. In the marque's favor were the sheer number of different models that had been produced over the company's relatively short span of production, and the strong reputation for excellence of certain machines, especially a number of Chief and Scout models.

Many of Indian's franchised dealers organized picnics, events and rides for their customers and although these events gradually faded from prominence others have taken their place. In more recent years Indian-only motorcycle events have been arranged by interested enthusiasts. In Massachusetts, John Marcoulier and Russell Longey started the Pioneer Valley Indian Rally. The inaugural event was held in 1991. The duo time the weekend – the third in July – to coincide with the annual Indian Day Rally in Springfield, Massachusetts, which is held in the grounds of the Indian Museum adjacent to the old Indian works. A ride out from the Pioneer Valley event to Springfield is one of the attractions there.

More recently the publishers of the enthusiast magazine, *Indian Motorcycle Illustrated*, have started Indian rallies at two of the biggest American bike events, Daytona and Sturgis, which are now primarily attended by Harley–Davidson riders. The second of these rallies is particularly noteworthy because JC 'Pappy' Hoel, who is credited with having started the massive Blackhills of Dakota event, was in fact originally an Indian dealer. It is a similar story elsewhere in the world where Indians were exported too. In Europe there is an annual Indian Rally that is hosted in a different country each year. It has been held in Austria, Belgium and Scotland for example. There are also Indian rallies in Australia. Racing is not forgotten either. Races for old bikes are run by a number of organizations including AHRMA – American Historic Racing Motorcycle Association – where Indians still run neck-and-neck with the Harleys. Just like the old days the rules let 45cu. in. (740cc) side-valves race against 30.50cu. in. (500cc) overhead-valves, meaning that in addition to arch-rival Harley–Davidsons there will also be BMWs, Nortons and Triumphs on the grid. One such event is held during the annual

Burning Blue
EAGLE HST
MT90-16
HEVEA MOTOR

Left: *Modified Indians from different eras: Leene's modern interpretation of a bobber (above); Jerry Turner's restored 1950s dirt-tracker (below). All the Century Chief (this page, below) shares with the original is its name. This is a modern attempt at a relaunch.*

Daytona, Florida, Bikeweek at the famous Speedway, where the pre-1940 race takes in five laps of the Daytona road course.

Max Bubeck is another motorcyclist with a lifetime's involvement with Indian motorcycles. He started riding in 1933 and set a speed of 135.8mph (218.5kph) on an Indian Chout (a Chief/Scout hybrid). He competed in 32 Greenhorn Enduros between 1937 and 1979. He won the event in 1947 on his Indian Four bought new that year and again in 1962 on an Indian V-twin. He re-enacted Cannonball Baker's epic trans-American ride at the age of 76 on a 1915 Indian V-twin. Baker had crossed the North American continent between San Diego, California, and New York City, New York, in 11 days, 12 hours and 10 minutes in 1914. He covered a distance of 3379 miles (5437km) before there were roads all the way between the two cities. Bubeck, an ardent enthusiast, set out to recreate the journey in 1993 following as closely as possible the route that Baker had taken. He made the journey in 14 days, 1 hour and 45 minutes, covering 2838 miles.

The trade aspect of Indians has shifted its emphasis in recent years. Where once there were franchised Indian dealers in towns around the USA these have passed into history and in their place have come specialist stores. The specialists are, in the main, stores that either restore old motorcycles generally or specialize solely in Indians. The fact that so many machines are now being restored has led to a demand for reproduction parts. Both cycle and mechanical parts are now being reproduced to original specifications. New Old Stock (NOS) parts are becoming more scarce with each passing year so that consumable parts need to be reproduced if motorcycles are to stay roadworthy and oil-tight. As a result, the specialist trade is growing annually, making it possible to restore an Indian motorcycle from little more than a frame, forks and set of engine cases. This explains why swapmeets are an important part of most social Indian gatherings. The old junk in one person's garage may be just the part another Indian enthusiast is looking for. Because the Indian marque produced such diverse models over its 52-year span it is now not uncommon to see a Powerplus, a 1950s Chief and an Indian vertical together at an historic meet. It is no secret that the Iron Redskins will ride proudly into the future.

1948 Indian Chief Chopper

This chopped Indian Chief was first bought by Tom Ryan from Connecticut in 1971 as an unfinished custom project. The long-forked chopper was in its heyday in that decade. Despite its non-standard appearance, most of the parts in its construction are stock parts. The paint scheme and extra chrome-plating make it look more radically altered than it actually is. The owner restored it to this condition in 1993.

Specification

Model
Indian Chief Chopper
Year
1948
Bore and stroke
3.25 × 4.4375in.
Displacement
73.62cu. in. (1206.4cc)
Bhp
40
Valve configuration
Side-valve
Top speed
85mph (137kph)
Fuel consumption
40mpg
Transmission
Three-speed
Gearchange
Hand-shift
Wheelbase
64in. (estimate)
Wheel diameter
Front: 19in.
Rear: 16in.
Frame type
Plunger raked
Forks
Extended girders
Weight
n/a

SHOEI

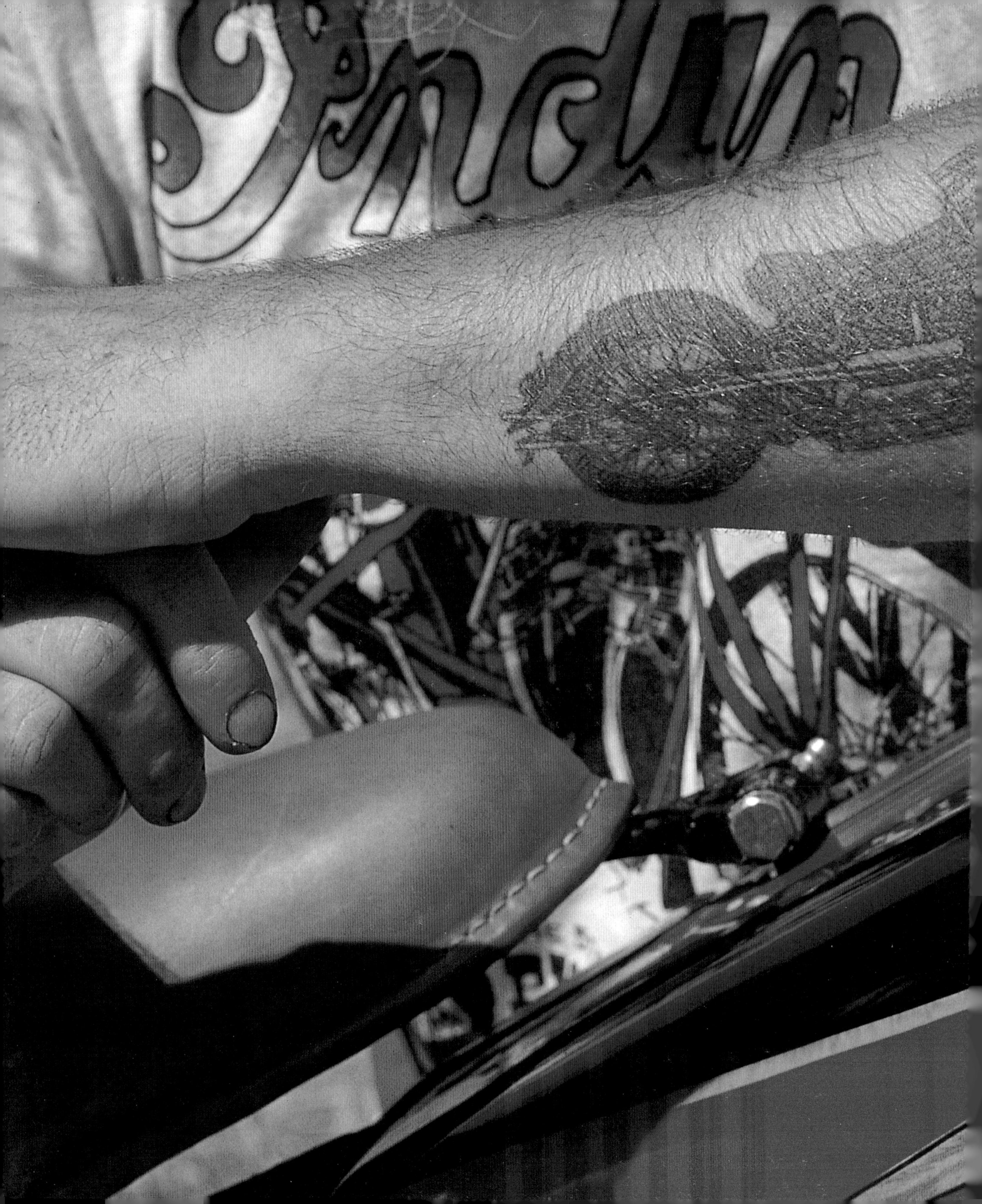